# Amazing Facts
# in
# U.S. History

BY
DON BLATTNER

COPYRIGHT © 2001 Mark Twain Media, Inc.

ISBN 1-58037-164-7

Printing No. CD-1385

Mark Twain Media, Inc., Publishers
Distributed by Carson-Dellosa Publishing Company, Inc.

# Table of Contents

# Table of Contents

# Introduction

There are two problems when studying American history. The first is that some of the most interesting or bizarre stories are ignored. These are the stories and facts that students would really enjoy, but they are just considered unimportant. Here are a few examples:

- When colonists wanted to clean the chimney, they dropped a live chicken down it.
- On his third voyage, Columbus thought he had discovered the Garden of Eden.
- President James Garfield was able to write in Greek with one hand while he wrote Latin with the other hand.
- President Grover Cleveland had a jaw made of rubber.
- Presidents Ulysses S. Grant, Gerald Ford, and William Clinton were all born with names other than the ones we know them by.
- Pioneers traveling west in wagon trains hated certain Indians, not because they attacked them, but because they had toll bridges the settlers needed to use.
- Santa Anna, the Mexican leader of the Alamo attack, helped invent chewing gum.
- Confederate General Richard Ewell thought he was a bird.

The second problem in studying American history is that many of the "facts" we have either learned in school or that have been passed down from one generation to another are either not true or cannot be documented. Some of them may have begun as a story someone told his or her grandchild, the grandchild passed it along, and eventually it was published and became part of America's folklore. Here are some examples:

- Pocahontas probably did not save John Smith from execution by the Indians.
- Betsy Ross probably did not design the first American flag.
- Paul Revere wasn't the only one to warn the American colonists that the English were arriving. And he didn't shout, "The British are coming."
- George Washington did not chop down a cherry tree when he was a child.

This book is designed as a series of quizzes that includes many strange facts of American history. It doesn't deal with all of the important issues that students learn in school. Instead, by revealing little-known facts, it gives a personal, intimate view of the people and events that have shaped America. The book is especially valuable as a pre-learning activity. Prior to studying a unit, one of the tests from this book should pique a student's interest, arouse his or her curiosity, and give a different perspective to what he or she is about to learn. It will be a springboard for discussion. Just as important as the facts and answers are the explanations after each quiz. The explanation of the correct answer gives elaborate details concerning these unusual historical facts. The answers and explanations are printed just after the questions so they can be duplicated and given to the students for further study.

In addition to the quizzes, there are puzzles and logic problems dealing with American history. Some are very easy, while others are quite difficult. Also, there are several sections called "A Mystery From History." These are historical mysteries that the students are invited to solve. They can solve the mystery by themselves, in groups, or the teacher may present the mystery as a 20-questions type of activity. In this case, the teacher would read the mystery to the class and the students would try to solve it by asking the teacher questions. The teacher can only answer "yes" or "no" to the questions.

Here's one other suggestion. Have your students start a class list of strange and unusual facts of history they find in their research. Print the list for your students at the end of the year.

Name: _____ Date: _____

# American Indians

Thousands of years before European explorers ventured into North America, someone else discovered the continents now known as North and South America. Their descendants were living on these continents centuries before European explorers arrived and were at the shore watching in wonder as strange boats filled with peculiarly-dressed men stepped ashore and claimed the land for themselves. The original explorers were named "Indians" by Columbus because he thought that he had landed in India. Eventually, he and subsequent explorers regarded these "Indians" as savages. While the Indians did not have the technology the Europeans had, they did, however, have religion, government, laws, and social structure, which we associate with civilized cultures.

Many people tend to think of Indians as one group of people. However, there were many different tribes and groups of Indians. Some groups shared beliefs or customs with others and some did not. In any case, the American Indian cultures are unique and fascinating.

Here are some strange and little-known facts about American Indians and their lives before Europeans came to America. Since there were so many diverse tribes in North America, the facts may refer to only one or a few of the tribes and not to all.

1. Which of the following did American Indians *not* burn for fuel.
   A. Wood
   B. Buffalo chips
   C. Fish
   D. Fire ants

2. A game invented by the Indians was similar to:
   A. Cowboys and Indians.
   B. Lacrosse.
   C. Baseball.
   D. Chinese checkers.

3. The Cree Indians used this as currency.
   A. Smoking pipes
   B. Gold coins
   C. Ponies
   D. Buffalo nickels

4. When was the final name of a Plains Indian generally given?
   A. When he became an adult
   B. At birth
   C. After death
   D. When he married

5. Whenever Natchez Indians went swimming, they always took along:
   A. Sun screen.
   B. Life preservers made of buffalo intestines.
   C. Ear plugs.
   D. Lifeguards.

Name:_____  Date:_____

6.  The word "Eskimo" is an Algonquian word that means:
    A. Blubber eaters.                      B. People who make pies.
    C. Ice people.                          D. Raw meat eaters.

7.  A Commanche man usually married:
    A. His cousins.                         B. The wife of those he killed.
    C. His first wife's younger sisters.    D. After signing a prenuptial agreement.

8.  The Mogollon tribe of the Southwest generally wore:
    A. Nothing.                             B. Kilts.
    C. Togas.                               D. Designer loin cloths.

9.  Who was swindled when the Canarsee Indians sold Manhattan Island to the Dutch for $24?
    A. The Dutch                            B. The Indians
    C. Neither                              D. Both

10. In order to stop a Plains Indian child from crying:
    A. It was spanked.                      B. Water was sometimes squirted up its nose.
    C. It was given a cloth soaked in honey. D. It was given a time out.

11. Pima Indians grew cotton which was woven by:
    A. London mills.                        B. Widows of the tribe.
    C. The women of the tribe.              D. The men of the tribe.

12. Natchez Indians placed board and clay pads around an infant's skull so they would have:
    A. Pointy heads.                        B. Strong necks.
    C. Good posture.                        D. A regal bearing.

13. Indians living on the northwest coast of America enjoyed eating this as a delicacy.
    A. Copra                                B. Eskimo pies
    C. Fish heads                           D. Moose hoof porridge

14. Today most Navajo Indians use blankets made and sold by:
    A. Pendleton Mills of Portland.         B. Navajo women.
    C. Navajo men.                          D. Wal-Mart.

15. Which kind of warfare did the Europeans *not* engage in when trying to eliminate the Indians?
    A. Armed conflict                       B. Search and destroy
    C. Jousting                             D. Germ Warfare

# American Indians—Answer Sheet

1. **D.** **Fire ants.** The candlefish (Thaleichthys) was a small fish so saturated with oil that it would burn. Strings of the candlefish tied together would provide light for the campground when it was dark.
2. **B.** **Lacrosse.**
3. **A.** **Smoking pipes.**
4. **C.** **After death.** A distinguished warrior was often given the privilege of naming a new child. For this service he was paid in horses. Names for Indians might often be changed several times during their lives. Their final names might even be given after their death because it was considered inappropriate or unsafe to utter the name of someone who had just died.
5. **D.** **Lifeguards.** The Natchez Indians enjoyed swimming, but they had lifeguards posted in order to keep the alligators away.
6. **D.** **Raw meat eaters.**
7. **C.** **His first wife's younger sisters.** If a woman was widowed, she married her deceased husband's brother.
8. **B.** **Kilts.**
9. **A.** **The Dutch.** Two Indian tribes lived on what is now Manhattan. One tribe occupied three-fourths of the Island and the other occupied one-fourth. Neither claimed ownership. So when Peter Minuit of the Dutch colonies offered to buy the Island from the Canarsees—the tribe that occupied one-fourth of the Island—they were eager to sell, since they didn't own it anyway. Incidentally, if the sale price of $24 had been invested at six percent interest and compounded annually, it would be worth over $70 billion in the year 2000.
10. **B.** **Water was sometimes squirted up its nose.** Plains Indian children were not usually scolded or punished. However, it was important for children not to cry or scream because this noise could alert an enemy. So whenever a child was screaming, water was often squirted up his nose in order to stop him from screaming.
11. **D.** **The men of the tribe.**
12. **A.** **Pointy heads.** It was considered attractive.
13. **C.** **Fish heads.** The heads of fish were split, dried, and allowed to rot before they were eaten as a delicacy.

14. **A.** **Pendleton Mills of Portland.** Blankets woven by Navajo women are so expensive today that most Navajos cannot afford them. Most use commercially-made machine-woven blankets made by Pendleton Mills in Portland, Oregon.
15. **C.** **Jousting.** On several occasions, the colonists gave unsuspecting Indians blankets and other items that had been used by smallpox victims (an early form of germ warfare).

Name: _____  Date: _____

# Columbus

Christopher Columbus, an Italian-born navigator sailing under a Spanish flag, is commonly given credit for discovering what we now call America. We know, of course, that American Indians were here when Columbus arrived and that Vikings and probably other Europeans had landed on the American shores before him. Even though Columbus was not the person to discover what is now known as the Americas, his voyages still remain heroic. We know that Columbus was in search of a westward route to Asia by sea, but the discoveries he made were more important and valuable than the route he was seeking. As a result of Columbus's voyages, the New World developed and became part of the European world.

See if you are able to discover some little-known facts about Christopher Columbus and his voyages. Read each of the following sentences and circle the letter before the correct answer.

1. When Columbus arrived in Cuba, he found the natives:
   A. Singing calypso tunes.            B. Building rafts to sail to America.
   C. Complaining about the heat.       D. Smoking Cuban cigars.

2. When some scholars heard of Columbus's adventures, studied his maps, and inspected the exotic plants, animals, and natives that he brought back from his voyage, they concluded that Columbus had found another continent. Columbus refused to believe this because he said if there were another continent:
   A. Marco Polo would have mentioned it.    B. It would be on the maps.
   C. The Bible would have revealed it.       D. It would have been found long ago.

3. After his first two voyages, Columbus came to believe that the earth was:
   A. Flat.                             B. Round.
   C. Square.                           D. Pear-shaped.

4. One of Columbus's shipmates was:
   A. Juan de Ponce de Leon.            B. Rocky Balboa.
   C. Leonardo di Caprio.               D. Ferdinand de Bull.

5. On his third voyage, Columbus thought that he might have discovered:
   A. A new continent.                  B. The Garden of Eden.
   C. Ohio.                             D. Canada.

4

Name: _____ Date: _____

6.  When Columbus returned from his third voyage he was wearing:
    A. Silken gowns.                          B. A velvet robe and feathered boa.
    C. Chains.                                D. Buckskin breeches and moccasins.

7.  From the original investment of $6,000 in Columbus's first voyage, Spain had a return in gold worth:
    A. $1,750,000.                            B. Nothing.
    C. $2.59.                                 D. $678,000,000.

8.  In his journal, which one of the following is *not* listed as one of Columbus's ships on his first voyage?
    A. Niña                                   B. Pinta
    C. Santa Maria                            D. La Capitana

9.  On Columbus's fourth voyage he was marooned for a year in Jamaica because his ships were:
    A. Sunk.                                  B. Rotted by shipworms.
    C. Stolen by pirates.                     D. Burned by hostile natives.

10. The captain of one of Columbus's ships, the Pinta, was named Martin Alonso Pinzon. He died two weeks after the voyage returned. In his memory, Pinzon's relatives:
    A. Sued Columbus.                         B. Erected a statue.
    C. Had a holiday named after him.         D. Had a city in Cuba named for him.

11. A ship's captain is required to keep a log of his journey. On Columbus's first voyage he kept:
    A. An accurate log.                       B. A phony log.
    C. An accurate and a phony log.           D. No log at all.

12. When Christopher Columbus died in 1506, he believed that he had discovered:
    A. A new continent.                       B. A new route to the East.
    C. The lost city of Atlantis.             D. Babylonia.

13. Queen Isabella, the Spanish Queen who provided Columbus with money for his voyage, was a Christian and expected everyone else to be a Christian as well. If she found someone in her kingdom who was not a very good Christian, she would have him burned at the stake. While he was burning, she would:
    A. Have choir boys sing.                  B. Shout, "This is just a taste of hell!"
    C. Have a prayer vigil.                   D. Have a street fair.

# Columbus—Answer Sheet

1. **D.** **Smoking Cuban Cigars.**
2. **C.** **The Bible would have revealed it.** At this time religious people believed that six-sevenths of the earth was composed of land and only one-sixth was ocean. This is hard for us to understand since we can look at maps and globes and see how big the ocean is. But in Columbus's day, people hadn't sailed very far from shore. They also believed that there were only three continents—Europe, Africa, and Asia. Asia was known as the Indies.
3. **D.** **Pear-shaped.** Columbus said that while he always agreed with Ptolemy, the Greek astronomer, and other scientists that the world was round, he decided that "it is not round as they describe but of the shape of a pear."
4. **A.** **Juan de Ponce de Leon.**
5. **B.** **The Garden of Eden.** He arrived at the Orinoco River in South America, which had four heads. He recalled that the Bible said that the Garden of Eden was the source of a river that split into four heads and that the Garden was located east of the point where the sun first appeared. Columbus wrote that the place he discovered was, "the earthly paradise whither no one can go but by God's permission."
6. **C.** **Chains.** Columbus and his brother, Bartholomew, were sent back to Spain in chains.
7. **A.** **$1,750,000.**
8. **C.** **Santa Maria.** Columbus's ships were called *Niña, Pinta* and the *La Capitana*, which means the flagship, according to Columbus's journal. His crew called the ship, *La Gallega,* which means The Galacian. The ship was built in Galicia. There is some evidence that the real name may have been the Mariagalante, which means flirtatious Mary. Santa Maria was the flagship for Columbus's second voyage.
9. **B.** **Rotted by shipworms.**
10. **A.** **Sued Columbus.** The relatives said that Columbus could not have made the voyage without the knowledge and skill of Pinzon. They maintained that Columbus and Pinzon had made a deal that everything earned by the voyage would be split equally between the two.

11. **C.** **An accurate and a phony log.** Columbus was afraid that if his crew actually knew how far they had sailed, they would be afraid and might mutiny. So while he kept an accurate log, which was important for future voyages, he also kept a phony log that showed that they had not sailed as far as they did. Strangely enough, he overestimated his speed so that the phony log proved to be more accurate than the one he thought was accurate.
12. **B.** **A new route to the East.**
13. **A.** **Have choir boys sing.** She wanted the sound of the choir singing to cover up the screaming of the person who was being burned.

Name: _____  Date: _____

# A Mystery from History
## COLUMBUS AND THE DISAPPEARING MOON

Columbus was now 51 years old, and he was sick. This, his fourth, and what would turn out to be his last, voyage was intended to be his redemption. He would prove to the world that he had found a new route to the East. He would be vindicated. But the problems encountered on this trip were even greater than the ones before. There was a terrible hurricane that damaged some of his ships. Columbus and his crew eventually made it to what is now Jamaica. Again his ships were damaged by a storm and the rest were rotted with shipworms. They could no longer be sailed. Columbus was stuck. Fortunately, the natives supplied him with food.

This worked for several months, but after a time the Jamaicans refused to supply Columbus with any more food. They wanted Columbus to leave. With no food, no way back to Spain and his men on the verge of mutiny, Columbus was at his wit's end, when he remembered something he had read. He went back into his cabin, consulted his charts, and had an idea.

Columbus arranged a meeting with the natives on the evening of February 29, 1504. When they were assembled, Columbus raised his arms and shouted. "Hear me. God is angry at you and your people. You have not treated Columbus, his son, well."

The Jamacians looked on in wonder. Was this another trick of this strange man who had already taken so much from their people?

"God has told me that as your punishment," Columbus continued, "he will take the moon out of the sky and make the night so dark that no man will be able to see. And then he will take away the sun! And your people will be left in darkness."

The natives shifted uneasily. Surely this was an idle threat. But still, they thought it wise not to take a chance and mock God.

Columbus again raised his arms and looked toward heaven. He spoke in a strange language and said things that the natives did not understand.

For several minutes, nothing happened and the natives began to relax, feeling this was just a trick of Columbus to get some more food. They were on the verge of attacking Columbus when something strange happened. One of the natives pointed to the moon. Was it his imagination, or did it look like the moon began to disappear? The other natives looked up and saw it too. They began to talk excitedly among themselves. As the moon gradually disappeared from the sky, the natives began to wail and moan. Some fell to the ground, screaming. They pleaded with Columbus to have God return their moon. They promised to give Columbus food and not to harm him.

"I will go back to my cabin and speak to God," Columbus said. He left and a while later, the moon began to reappear in the sky. Columbus returned and the natives were joyous and immediately began supplying Columbus and his men with food again. Eventually, Columbus and his men were rescued.

How could this happen? How did Columbus make the moon disappear? Did he really pray to God, or did he know some kind of trick to make it appear as if the moon disappeared?

Name:_____  Date:_____

# Explorers

     The discovery of the Americas was just an accident. Explorers discovered this "new world" while sailing westward across the Atlantic Ocean in an attempt to reach the East. After Columbus and Vespucci, many people in Europe became interested in these new lands. Several countries sent explorers to look for a passage to the East, to build colonies, or to find riches. These explorers had many adventures and greatly affected the native population they found. Do you know the strange and usual facts concerning the following explorers? Read each of the following sentences and circle the letter before the correct answer.

1.  Who discovered the Hudson River?
     A. Giovanni da Verrazano          B. Henry Hudson
     C. Samuel Hudson                D. John Cabot

2.  The first English vessel to reach the New World was commanded by the:
     A. English.                     B. French.
     C. Spanish.                   D. Italians.

3.  The first French vessel to reach the New World was commanded by the:
     A. English.                     B. French.
     C. Spanish.                   D. Italians.

4.  The first Spanish vessel to reach the New World was commanded by the:
     A. English.                     B. French.
     C. Spanish.                   D. Italians.

5.  Who was the first known European to visit America?
     A. Christopher Columbus         B. Juan Valdez
     C. Bjarni Heriulfson             D. Leif Erikson

6.  Henry Hudson was:
     A. English.                     B. Italian.
     C. Dutch.                     D. Spanish.

7.  In 1536, Richard Hore organized a _____ to the New World.
     A. Pleasure cruise            B. Scientific expedition
     C. Invasion                   D. Hunting expedition

8.  When de Soto and his men landed in Florida in 1539 to explore the land, he brought along 13 hogs. They were to be used for food as well as for:
     A. Pets.                        B. Gifts to Indians.
     C. Racing.                     D. Protection from snakes.

Name: _____     Date: _____

9. On his first voyage to the South Pacific in 1768, Captain Cook lost 41 of his 98 crew to scurvy, which is a disease caused by a lack of vitamin C. By 1795 it was discovered that by eating citrus, scurvy could be eliminated. As a result, all British Navy ships provided a ration of:
   A. Rum.                                           B. GatorAde.
   C. Kool Aid.                                      D. Lemon juice.

10. Because of the special diet supplement used to prevent scurvy, English sailors were called:
   A. Rum Heads.                                     B. Limeys.
   C. Gator Goats.                                   D. Lemon Drop Kids.

11. Pizarro had spent a year conquering the coastal settlements of Peru when he encountered Atahualpa, the Inca emperor. Pizarro captured Atahualpa, and slaughtered 2,000 of Atahualpa's men because Atahualpa would not:
   A. Give him gold.                                 B. Give him food.
   C. Become a Christian.                            D. Validate his parking ticket.

12. In 1501, at age 26, Balboa joined a Spanish expedition to South America in order to gain wealth and fame. He eventually ended up on the island of Hispaniola:
   A. Raising pigs.                                  B. Teaching Spanish to Indians.
   C. Selling tourist maps.                          D. Hunting snipe.

13. Once Balboa reached the Pacific Ocean and claimed it and all adjacent lands for Spain, his men found gold and pearls, which he sent back to King Ferdinand of Spain along with word of his great discoveries in the name of Spain. Eventually Balboa was:
   A. Named admiral of the Spanish Navy.             B. Given a pension for life.
   C. Beheaded.                                      D. Emperor of the Panamanian Indians.

14. Before Cortez was sent to conquer the Aztecs, he was:
   A. A law student.                                 B. An Olympic athlete.
   C. An importer.                                   D. A flamenco dancer.

15. Which of the following did Spanish explorers generally *not* take on their voyages?
   A. Priests                                        B. Dogs
   C. Cats                                           D. Canaries

# Explorers—Answer Sheet

1. **A.** **Giovanni da Verrazano.** Henry Hudson did not discover the Hudson River, Hudson Strait, or Hudson Bay.
2. **D.** **Italians.** John Cabot. (Giovanni Caboto)
3. **D.** **Italians.** The Italian, Giovanni da Verrazano.
4. **D.** **Italians.** Christopher Columbus (Cristoforo Columbo).
5. **C.** **Bjarni Heriulfson.** Bjarni Heriulfson sighted North America about 985–986. Some believe Irish seamen reached the United States in the ninth or tenth century, in boats called curraghs. Others believe a Welshman named Modoc established a colony and taught the local Indians how to speak Welsh.
6. **A.** **English.** Henry Hudson was English, not Dutch.
7. **A.** **Pleasure Cruise.** In 1536, Richard Hore organized a pleasure cruise to the New World. Pleasure cruises or tourist cruises to the Mediterranean were common during this period, although they were advertised as "pilgrimages." Hore thought a pleasure cruise to the New World would be very profitable for him. He hired two ships and advertised that he was organizing a sightseeing tour across the ocean. About 120 people signed up to participate in this adventure. When the ships arrived in Newfoundland, they ran out of food and other provisions. The crew and passengers began to starve. They tried living off of the land but were unable to. They even resorted to cannibalism. When French ships came into the harbor, the starving Englishmen captured the ships and sailed back to England.
8. **D.** **Protection from snakes.** Hogs are very good at killing snakes.
9. **D.** **Lemon juice.**
10. **B.** **Limeys.**
11. **C.** **Become a Christian.** When Atahualpa refused to convert to Christianity or to accept the Spanish king as his sovereign, he was seized and his warriors were killed. Atahualpa's subjects delivered an estimated $30 million worth of gold and silver for the release of their emperor; however, Atahualpa was executed eight months after his capture.
12. **A.** **Raising pigs.**
13. **C.** **Beheaded.** The King learned of Balboa's discovery of the Pacific Ocean and appointed him to serve under Pedrarias Davila as governor of Panama. Pedrarias was jealous of Balboa's popularity. He accused Balboa of treason and had him arrested, tried, and beheaded.
14. **A.** **A law student.**
15. **D.** **Canaries.** Priests were taken to convert the natives. Cats were needed for the rats on the ship. Dogs were used to attack Indians. It is estimated that one dog was as effective as eight men in subduing Indians.

Name: _____  Date: _____

# Explorers Puzzle

Using the clues given below, fill in the following grid with the names of explorers who sailed to the Americas. If you fill in the grid correctly, you will be able to read down the circles and learn what all of the explorers had in common.

1.
2.
3.
4.
5.
6.
7.
8.
9.
10.
11.

## Clues

1. First Spanish explorer to see the Mississippi River
2. Frenchman who was the European discoverer of the St. Lawrence River
3. Italian-born navigator who sailed for Spain; most people give him credit for discovering America
4. The Spanish conqueror of Mexico
5. Italian navigator and explorer who sailed in the service of England; his voyages made it possible for the English claims to North America
6. The Italian explorer and navigator who was the first to describe the Western Hemisphere as an unknown continent rather than as a part of Asia; the New World was named for him
7. Portuguese explorer who led the first expedition to circumnavigate the world
8. Spanish conquistador who secured Peru for Spain by conquering the Incas
9. Portuguese navigator who discovered the Cape of Good Hope and proved there was a route to India around the southern point of Africa
10. French fur trader who is credited as the European explorer of the lower Mississippi
11. English-born navigator who undertook several voyages in search of the Northwest Passage for the Dutch and the English; there is a famous bay named after him

Name: _____ Date: _____

# Exploration Cube Puzzle

Many of the explorers who came to the "new world" had a similar goal. That goal is hidden in the puzzle below. The answer to the puzzle begins with the circled letter (N) and ends with the other circled letter (E). Follow a vertical, horizontal, or diagonal path from the first letter to the last and the answer will be spelled out. Do not cross the path you have already made. Each letter is used only once. You can use the blanks shown below to record your answer. The first and last letters are already filled in for you.

| S | S | A | G |
|---|---|---|---|
| O | A | P | (E) |
| R | (N) | S | T |
| T | H | W | E |

N __ __ __ __ __ __ __ __    __ __ __ __ __ __ E

# The Fountain of Youth

Ponce de Leon was not successful in locating the Fountain of Youth in Florida because it did not exist. But what if there were such a thing as a Fountain of Youth and you discovered it? This is the plot of a short story you are to write. Imagine you are on a camping trip in Florida and you become separated from your group. As you search for a way to return, you discover a beautiful and refreshing spring or fountain. It turns out to be the Fountain of Youth, and nobody knows about it but you. What would you do?

Here are some of the things you might want to include in your story:

- Background of where you are, why you are there, and how you got separated from the group.
- The scene where you discover the Fountain of Youth. How do you know what it is?
- Do you tell anyone about your discovery? Why? How do you keep it a secret?
- What do you do about your discovery? Buy the land it is on? Sell the water? Keep it for yourself and your family? Donate it to the government?
- What happens as a result of your discovery and decision? For example, if no one would grow old, how would that affect society and the world?

Name: _____ Date: _____

# A Mystery From History

## THE SPANISH GOLD MYSTERY

Variations of the following conundrum have been told for centuries. We have our doubts that it ever happened, but it is a good puzzle and one you might enjoy trying to solve.

Throughout the history of humankind, gold has been treasured as a standard for value. There is evidence that gold was used in decorative arts as early as 9000 B.C. Even those civilizations that developed little or no use of other metals prized gold for its beauty and value. So it was no surprise that when Spanish explorers came to the newly-discovered land, one of their primary goals was to find gold. This valuable metal was not only sought because it would enrich the explorers and their countries, but it would also make them famous and powerful.

This lust for gold tempted the Spanish explorers so much that they sometimes would believe the most outlandish stories American Indians would tell them about gold and then make foolish decisions based on these stories. One of these explorers was Coronado.

Francisco Vazquez de Coronado was a Spanish explorer who is now noted for exploring the American southwest. In February 1540, however, Coronado's goal was not just to explore, but to look for gold. Indians had told him that somewhere in the interior of the continent were very wealthy cities. These cities were called the "Seven Cities of Cibola." They are sometimes simply called the "Seven Cities of Gold."  The Indians said the cities were so rich that the people lived in very large houses made of stone and they had knives, spoons, and other utensils made of gold and silver. Coronado believed these stories and set out to become rich and famous.

For three years Coronado and his men pushed forward in their quest. Some went into what is now Kansas, and others saw the Grand Canyon. But they found little gold. Coronado decided to return to Mexico and accept failure. However, there are some who tell the story of three of Coronado's men who did not give up and refused to return with Coronado. While the truthfulness of this story cannot be verified, it has been told around thousands of campfires for hundreds of years.

It is said that the three Spaniards pushed forward until they found a small village that did have a small amount of gold. While it would not be enough to satisfy Coronado and his many men, it was certainly enough to make the three rich. The Indians of this village were no match for the superior weapons of the Spaniards. The conquistadors easily killed several Indians and took their gold. Then they selected three young, strong Indians to lead them back to Mexico and to carry their loot. They also brought along a small canoe in case they needed to cross a river or stream.

The Spaniards were happy. They had succeeded where Coronado had failed. They talked endlessly about their good fortune and how they would celebrate when they returned to Mexico. But all the while they were celebrating, they kept a close watch on the Indians. They knew that, if given a chance, the Indians would kill them, take the gold, and return to their village.

All went well for several days, and the conquistadors began to relax, until one day they came to a river to cross. It was apparent that the only way across the river was to use the dugout canoe they had brought with them. The problem was, the canoe could only hold two men at a time. The conquistadors needed to get all six people and all of the gold across the river. The Spaniards realized that if two Indians were alone with one Spaniard, the Indians could easily overpower him and take the gold. The Spaniards had to figure out a way to get the gold and all six people across the river safely. How could they do it?

Name: _____ Date: _____

# Pocahontas and Jamestown

The famous American Indian princess Pocahontas was born around 1595. Her clan name was Matoaka. Pocahontas was the daughter of Powhatan, chief of the Powhatan confederacy in the Tidewater region of Virginia. Not only was she loved by her tribe, the colonists at Jamestown said she was beautiful and intelligent.

Pocahontas most likely saw white men for the first time in 1607 when Englishmen arrived in Jamestown. Most school books tell of the first meeting of Pocahontas and John Smith. According to the legend, Smith was leading an expedition in December 1607 when he was captured by Indians. Eventually, he was taken to Chief Powhatan. Smith said that at first he was welcomed by the great chief and offered food. Then he was attacked and stretched out on two flat stones. According to Smith, the Indians were ready to beat him to death when a young Indian girl rushed in, threw herself over him to protect him from the clubs, and saved his life. The girl, of course, was Pocahontas. She was about twelve years old at the time. The Chief was so moved that he spared Smith's life and adopted him as his son. That's the famous story.

Pocahontas and Smith became friends. She was a frequent visitor to Jamestown. She delivered messages between her tribe and the colonists. She would also accompany the Indian men as they came to Jamestown with furs and food to trade for tools and trinkets. It is also recorded that Pocahontas helped the colonists by persuading her father to provide food to the starving colonists at Jamestown.

Pocahontas married an English colonist, became a Christian, took a Christian name, and had a child. She was apparently a very charming woman who not only won the hearts of the English colonists, but delighted those in London society as well.

Here are some strange and little-known facts about the Indian princess Pocahontas. Read each of the following sentences and circle the letter before the correct answer.

1. John Smith was forced by Indians to stretch out while they stood above him with clubs. They were about to execute him when Pocahontas rushed in and laid her own head upon his to save him from death. This execution was probably:
   A. A sacrifice for crops.               B. Only a mock execution.
   C. Revenge for counterfeiting wampum.   D. Sport.

2. Whom did Pocahontas marry?
   A. John Smith                           B. John Rolfe
   C. John Unitas                          D. Roger Smith

3. When Pocahontas was baptized, she was renamed:
   A. Tammy Sue.                           B. Rebecca.
   C. Little Dove.                         D. Bambi.

4. When Pocahontas died, she was:
   A. 87 years old.                        B. 46 years old.
   C. 22 years old.                        D. 16 years old.

14

Name:_____ Date:_____

5.  John Rolfe and Pocahontas decided to marry. However, Rolfe would not marry her unless she:
    A. Stopped calling him Kemo Sabe.          B. Gave up lacrosse.
    C. Threw away smelly deerskin dresses.     D. Became a Christian.

6.  When Pocahontas saw Captain John Smith, the old friend she had not seen for eight years, she called him:
    A. Father.                                 B. Captain.
    C. John.                                   D. Skippy.

7.  Thomas Rolfe, the son of John Rolfe and Pocahontas, became:
    A. Chief of the Powhatan Tribe.            B. Owner of a used pony lot.
    C. An Indian scout.                        D. A wealthy landowner.

8.  Thomas Rolfe, the son of John Rolfe and Pocahontas, went to war against:
    A. The French.                             B. The English.
    C. His mother's tribe.                     D. The Cleveland Indians.

9.  Pocahontas had a sister named:
    A. Pokeyli'lpuppi.                         B. Cleopatra.
    C. Sasquatch.                              D. Debbie.

10. For the first ten years of their lives, the only thing the Indian children who lived close to Jamestown wore was:
    A. Loincloths.                             B. Lamb's wool.
    C. Deerskin.                               D. Bear grease and juice.

11. The Indians who lived close to Jamestown shaved their heads on the right side:
    A. So they would be more attractive.       B. So it wouldn't get tangled in bowstrings.
    C. To get on their parents' nerves.        D. To show they weren't married.

12. In April of 1607, settlers from England reached land and sailed up a river that they named "James" in honor of their king. After they sailed about 30 miles from the mouth of the river, they landed and founded a colony they named Jamestown. The spot was chosen because:
    A. The water supply was good.              B. It provide protection from Indians.
    C. It reminded them of England.            D. It provided protection from pirates.

# Pocahontas and Jamestown—Answer Sheet

1. **B.** **Only a mock execution.** There is no evidence that this actually happened. We only have John Smith's story that it occurred. He didn't even tell the story until quite a bit after it supposedly happened. We do know that a mock "execution and salvation" ceremony was traditional for this tribe. So in all probability, the execution and Pocahontas's brave actions were a part of that ritual.

2. **B.** **John Rolfe.** We have all heard the story of Pocahontas and John Smith so often we tend to believe that she married Smith. Actually she married John Rolfe, another colonist. Another little-known fact is that Rolfe was Pocahontas's second marriage. She married an Indian named Kocoum when she was about fourteen years old. We don't know if Kocoum died or if they were divorced.

3. **B.** **Rebecca.**

4. **C.** **22 years old.**

5. **D.** **Became a Christian.** John Rolfe was a very religious man and could not decide if he wanted to marry a heathen Indian.

6. **A.** **Father.** When Pocahontas was in London, she saw Captain John Smith. She had not seen him for eight years, so she thought he was dead. According to Smith's account of the meeting, Pocahontas was so overcome with emotion when she saw him that at first she could not speak. When she was able to speak again, they reminisced and at one point she called him "father." He objected and she said, "Were you not afraid to come into my father's Countrie, and caused feare in him and all of his people and here I should call you father: I tell you I will, and you shall call mee childe, and so I will be for ever and ever your Countrieman." This was their last meeting.

7. **D.** **Wealthy landowner.** He inherited not only his father's 400-acre plantation, but also thousands of acres from his grandfather, Chief Powhatan. In fact, if he had chosen to, he could have become chief of the Powhatan tribe.

8. **C.** **His mother's tribe.** The Powhatan tribe massacred 347 colonists, including Thomas's father, John Rolfe. The tribe was led by Chief Opechancanough, who was Thomas's uncle.

9. **B.** **Cleopatra.**

10. **D.** **Bear grease and juice.**

11. **B.** **So it wouldn't get tangled in bowstrings.**

12. **D.** **It provided protection from pirates.** The spot was so far from the mouth of the river, the settlers felt that the area would be safe from pirates. The place was a swampy, low area full of mosquitoes. It was not a good spot for a settlement. The weather was hot all summer, and the water supply was not good. The settlers had not chosen very wisely.

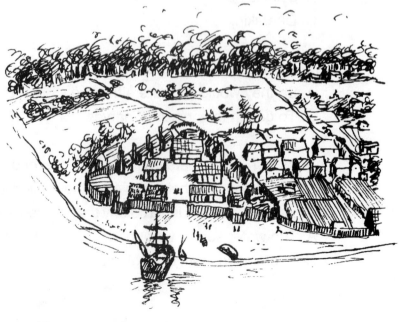

16

Name: _____ Date: _____

# The First Thanksgiving

Americans tend to think that the idea of a thanksgiving day originated in America. In fact, days of thanksgiving have occurred throughout history in many different lands. Whenever a group of people were thankful for something, they celebrated with prayers of thanks. In the United States, however, Thanksgiving is an annual holiday celebrated on the fourth Thursday in November. This holiday had its beginnings with a three-day feast and prayers celebrated by the Plymouth colonists in 1621. Most people do not realize that an earlier thanksgiving was offered in prayer alone by members of the Berkeley plantation near present-day Charles City, Virginia, on December 4, 1619.

How much do you know about the celebration we refer to as the first Thanksgiving? Read the following questions and circle the letter that represents the best answer.

1.  One of the main reasons the Pilgrims had autumnal feasts was to:
    A. Befriend Indians.               B. Celebrate survival.
    C. Socialize.                      D. Get fat.

2.  At this feast, napkins were used to clean fingers and to:
    A. Keep away flies.                B. Pick up hot food.
    C. Remove lipstick.                D. Protect shirts.

3.  Guests took the food they wished from each serving dish and ate it immediately, or put it on trenchers. Trenchers were plates made of:
    A. Wood.                           B. Porcelain.
    C. Metal.                          D. Deer skin.

4.  Which of the following items were *not* used at the first Thanksgiving?
    A. Knives                          B. Forks
    C. Spoons                          D. Napkins

5.  When the Pilgrims said they planted corn, they were referring to:
    A. Maize.                          B. Wheat.
    C. Corn.                           D. Barley.

6.  Which president first issued a proclamation making Thanksgiving a national holiday?
    A. Washington                      B. Jefferson
    C. Lincoln                         D. Grant

Name: _____ Date: _____

7. Which one of the following foods was probably *not* served at the first Thanksgiving?
   A. Turkey
   B. Ham
   C. Swan
   D. Eel

8. What did the Indians and Pilgrims probably *not* share at the first Thanksgiving?
   A. Plates
   B. Stories
   C. Food
   D. Prayers

9. Although we consider the Pilgrims' 1621 celebration as the first Thanksgiving, the first recorded act of thanksgiving by Europeans on this continent was celebrated in:
   A. Florida.
   B. Virginia.
   C. Canada.
   D. Mexico.

10. Pilgrims considered Thanksgiving as a day of:
    A. Feasting.
    B. Celebration.
    C. Fasting.
    D. Dancing.

11. Which game was probably *not* played at the 1621 Thanksgiving?
    A. Archery
    B. Shooting
    C. Football
    D. Racing

12. Who served the Pilgrims and Indians at the 1621 Thanksgiving?
    A. Indian women
    B. Pilgrim women
    C. Self-served
    D. Waitresses

13. The Pilgrims called the famous celebration of 1621:
    A. Harvest Home.
    B. Thanksgiving.
    C. Party Time.
    D. Feasting.

14. When Governor Bradford invited chief Masasoit and his brother to the feast, he was surprised when they arrived with:
    A. War bonnets.
    B. Wine.
    C. Ninety friends.
    D. Pumpkin pie.

15. After 1621, the Pilgrims celebrated the feast:
    A. Monthly.
    B. Annually.
    C. Occasionally.
    D. Never again.

# The First Thanksgiving—Answer Sheet

1. **D.   Get fat.** Some of the food colonists grew or trapped could not be kept or preserved. One of the best ways to store food for the winter was in the form of fat.
2. **B.   Pick up hot food.**
3. **A.   Wood.** They shared their plate with someone else. They were called trencher mates.
4. **B.   Forks.**
5. **B.   Wheat.**
6. **A.   Washington.** The first national Thanksgiving Day was proclaimed by President George Washington and celebrated on November 26, 1789. It was President Abraham Lincoln who made Thanksgiving an annual holiday in 1863. He set the date of the holiday on the last Thursday in November. This date was probably chosen because it was roughly the date that the Mayflower anchored at Cape Cod. (According to the Gregorian calendar. The pilgrims, who were using the Julian calendar, actually anchored on November 11.) Today, Thanksgiving is celebrated on the fourth Thursday of November. This date was set by President Franklin D. Roosevelt and approved by Congress in 1941.
7. **B.   Ham.** The Pilgrims probably did not have pigs. Here are some of the foods available for the feast. It is likely that many of them were served in 1621: Meat: venison (deer). Fish: bass, bluefish, herring, shad, and eel. Seafood: clams, lobsters, mussels, and oysters. Fowl: duck, crane, goose, partridge, swan, turkey, and possibly eagles. Grain: wheat flour, Indian corn, and corn meal. Fruit: (dried) blueberries, cherries, gooseberries, grapes, plums, raspberries, and strawberries. Vegetables: beans, leeks, onions, peas, and squashes. Nuts: acorns, chestnuts, hickory nuts, and walnuts.
8. **D.   Prayers.**
9. **D.   Mexico.** On April 30th, 1598, an expedition arrived on the banks of the Rio Grande in Nuevo, Mexico, which is close to what is now El Paso, Texas. The colonists suffered hardships and deprivations as they headed north. Then, on the banks of the Rio Grande, they found wildlife and fish, and they feasted. There were prayers of thanksgiving.
10. **C.   Fasting.** To the Pilgrims, a day of thanksgiving was one of fasting and prayer. They celebrated a day of thanksgiving whenever something good happened; for example, when a drought ended, a battle was won, or there was something to be thankful for.
11. **C.   Football.**
12. **C.   Self-served.**
13. **A.   Harvest Home.**
14. **C.   Ninety friends.**
15. **D.   Never again.**

19

Name: _____ Date: _____

# First Thanksgiving Meal Grid

What kind of food did the Pilgrims eat at the first Thanksgiving? Some of the foods are listed below. What is surprising is not only what they did eat, but what they did not eat. The Pilgrims most likely did not have sweet potatoes, potatoes, or yams. Corn on the cob was not served because Indian corn was only good for making cornmeal, not eating on the cob. There was no popcorn, oranges, apples, apple cider, cranberry sauce, pumpkin pie or whipped cream.

Here's a different kind of puzzle. Shown below is a list of the some of the foods that were served at what we call the first Thanksgiving. You are to fill in the grid with the foods. It is not as difficult as it appears. All you need to do is count the squares in order to see where the words will fit, but you may choose to use a pencil, in the event you need to erase and try a new word.

| THREE LETTERS | FOUR LETTERS | FIVE LETTERS | SIX LETTERS | SEVEN LETTERS |
|---|---|---|---|---|
| COD | CORN | CLAMS | TURKEY | OYSTERS |
| EEL | DEER | GOOSE | ACORNS | MUSSELS |
| | BASS | HONEY | GRAPES | WALNUTS |
| | DUCK | CRANE | SQUASH | |
| | SWAN | | | |

Name: _____ Date: _____

# The Colonies
## GENERAL FACTS

When we speak of the American colonies, we are referring to a span of time in America's history that lasts almost 200 years. It starts in 1607, with the establishment of the first colony, and ends in 1783, at the end of the revolution. There are three periods that can be studied during this time span. The first is the period of *settlement*. During this period, which lasted from 1607 until 1675, the colonies struggled with problems of survival and establishing settlements. The second is the period of *organization*. During this period, which lasted from 1675 until 1750, the colonies began to mature, gain power, and solve many governmental problems. The third period the colonies experienced, which lasted from 1750 until 1783, was the period of *revolution*. During this period, Europeans tried to exert their power over the colonies in the *French and Indian War* and in the *Revolutionary War*. This section will deal with the first two periods. The revolutionary period will be dealt with later.

Given below are strange and unusual facts concerning the colonial period. Read each of the following sentences and circle the letter before the correct answer.

1.  Until 1796, the state of Tennessee was known as:
    A. Cumberland.                          B. Washington.
    C. Franklin.                            D. Westphalia.

2.  If the colonists wanted to clean a chimney, they would put a broom up the chimney or:
    A. Use a chimney brush.                 B. Drop a live chicken down it.
    C. Use a stick wrapped in cloth.        D. Lower a child through it.

3.  In 1783, the best-selling book was:
    A. *The Holy Bible.*                    B. *Webster's American Spelling Book.*
    C. *The Sorcerer's Apprentice.*         D. *The Hairy Potter.*

4.  A common snack food in early America was:
    A. Bouillon cubes.                      B. Maize chips.
    C. Dried fish strips.                   D. Bear claws.

5.  In an effort to find a good way to light their homes, American colonists discovered that excellent candles could be made from:
    A. Sap from the wax birch tree.         B. The fruit of a squat bush.
    C. Ear wax.                             D. Gasoline.

6.  The first Bible to be printed in America was printed in what language?
    A. English                              B. Sign language
    C. Latin                                D. Algonquian Indian

Name:_____  Date:_____

7.  In the latter part of the 18th century, Phillis Wheatley became Boston's poetess laureate.
    Phillis Wheatley was:
    A. A wealthy socialite.                     B. A slave.
    C. An Algonquian Indian.                    D. Illiterate.

8.  The original Liberty Bell was made in:
    A. Pennsylvania.                            B. Paris.
    C. London.                                  D. Liberia.

9.  The Liberty Bell was given its name in honor of:
    A. America's Independence.                  B. Slaves seeking their freedom.
    C. Liberty Belle, a well-known dancer.      D. Victory in the French and Indian War.

10. When a colonial child wrote a letter to his father, he would address him as:
    A. Honorable Sir.                           B. Dear Daddy.
    C. Beloved Master.                          D. Hi, Pop.

11. In trained hands, which kind of weapons were most efficient in their ability to kill more
    enemies quickly and accurately?
    A. Guns                                     B. Bows and arrows
    C. Lances                                   D. Knives

12. During the 1600s, Harvard ranked students based on a guess of the student's academic
    performance. Later, class rank was determined by:
    A. Academic excellence.                     B. The alphabetical order of their names.
    C. Family status.                           D. Attendance.

13. Those who could not afford a horse for themselves:
    A. Sometimes shared one with others.        B. Took a trolly.
    C. Went to Hertz Rent-A-Nag.                D. Never went anyplace.

14. Until the 18th century, New Englanders spoke with a(n):
    A. English accent.                          B. Dutch accent.
    C. German accent.                           D. Southern accent.

# The Colonies: General Facts—Answer Sheet

1.  **C.**  **Franklin.**
2.  **B.**  **Drop a live chicken down it.**
3.  **B.**  ***Webster's American Spelling Book.***
4.  **A.**  **Bouillon cubes.** Stock from beef or veal was boiled down to a hard jelly. These hard jelly cakes didn't spoil. They were particularly good for trappers and hunters who could nibble on them as they traveled during the 1700s.
5.  **B.**  **The fruit of a squat bush.** Colonists discovered that high-quality candles could be made from the fruit of a squat bush. They would pick the grayish bayberries, crush, and boil them. It was necessary for them to skim the fat several times before it was refined. Bayberry candles were superior and treasured because so many berries were needed and it took so much work to make them.
6.  **D.**  **Algonquian Indian.** John Eliot, an American who was called the "Apostle to the Indians," translated the Bible into Algonquian Indian. It was the first Bible to be printed in America. It took three years to print it on Harvard's college press.
7.  **B.**  **A slave.** When she was seven, she was purchased by John Wheatley, a tailor. His wife realized that Phillis was very intelligent and taught her to read and write. She began writing poetry that everyone found impressive. When her mistress died, Phillis was set free.
8.  **C.**  **London.** The Liberty Bell was cast in London in 1752.
9.  **B.**  **Slaves seeking their freedom.** The bell was ordered in 1751, cast in London and arrived in Philadelphia in August 1752. It was cracked while being tested, was melted down, and a second bell was cast in April 1753, but this one was also defective. A third bell was cast in June of that year by the firm of Pass and Stowe in Philadelphia. On June 7, 1753, the third bell was hung in the tower of Independence Hall.

    While the bell was in the Philadelphia statehouse in 1776, it was not rung while the Declaration of Independence was being signed, as tradition says. In 1777, during the American Revolution, British troops occupied Philadelphia. The bell was removed from the tower and taken to Allentown, Pennsylvania for safekeeping. It was returned to Philadelphia and replaced in Independence Hall in 1778. In 1835 it cracked. Tradition says that it cracked as it was being tolled for the death of Chief Justice John Marshall. It is not clear if this is true or not.

    In 1828, Philadelphia tried to sell the bell as scrap, but no one wanted it. The first record anyone can find of the bell being referred to as the "Liberty Bell" was in a pamphlet in 1839. According to the pamphlet, the bell was meant to symbolize freedom of black slaves. The pamphlet was given out at an antislavery rally.
10.  **A.**  **Honorable Sir.** Letters were very formal, even when written to close family members.
11.  **B.**  **Bows and arrows.** Early guns took so long to load and fire that in trained hands, bows and arrows were twelve times more efficient than guns.
12.  **C.**  **Family status.** During the 1600s, Harvard ranked students based on a guess of the student's academic performance. Later, class rank was determined by family status. Yale also used family status as a method of ranking their students, but eventually decided to rank them according to the alphabet.

# The Colonies: General Facts—Answer Sheet

13. **A.** **Sometimes shared one with others.** Horseback riding was a common method of travel in the colonies. Those who could not afford a horse for themselves sometimes shared one with others. They used a method called *ride and tie*.

    Here's how it would work. One person would ride the horse for a mile or so, and then get off, tie the horse up, and continue walking. Then, another person who had been walking would get on the horse and would ride ahead for a mile or so. He, in turn, would then tie up the horse and continue walking.

14. **D.** **Southern accent.** The Southern accent was popular in America until the eighteenth century.

Name:_____    Date:_____

# Thirteen Colonies Puzzle

The original thirteen colonies enjoyed their independence. They not only wanted to be independent from England, they valued their independence from each of the other colonies. Eventually, however, the colonies did band together for a common cause. Their cooperative efforts developed something that still exists today. Shown below, on the left, is a list of the original thirteen colonies. You can see the letters have been scrambled. Unscramble the letters and place them in the spaces to the right of each. When you are finished, you will be able to read down the circles and discover what the original thirteen colonies developed.

1.  TEMAHSAUSCSTS

2.  NIRIVIAG

3.  DORHE NLAISD

4.  NHORT ORNLICAA

5.  ORGAGEI

6.  EAWDAREL

7.  WNE RKYO

8.  WNE SPHAMIRHE

9.  TUSOH ROCALINA

10. RYMANDLA

11. CTCOICUNENT

12. EWN YSEJER

13. LVANPNSYIENA

Name: _____ Date: _____

# Sports in the Colonies Logic Problem

Sports were different in the various colonies. The colonists of New England considered pleasure and fun to be sinful, so many sports were forbidden. In fact, there were strict laws against sports in some of the New England colonies. On the other hand, the settlers in the Southern Colonies did not have these strict laws concerning sports and pleasure. In the Southern Colonies, people not only participated in sports and games, they occasionally enjoyed betting on sports. From the clues given below, can you figure out how much money each person lost, on which type of sporting event, and in what months of the year?

Solving this problem is fun but challenging. All the information you need to solve the problem is given either in the introduction or in the clues. In addition to using the clues, you must also use logic to solve the problem. In order to solve the problem, you may use the solution chart on the next page. Write "yes" in the appropriate box on the chart when you discover a correct answer and "no" when you are sure that the box represents an incorrect answer. Sometimes as you work through the problem and fill out the solution chart, you may get stumped and need to guess at an answer. If you do guess, you can test the guess to see if it would work out with the clues you were given. If you discover your guess is incorrect, you can always change it on the solution chart.

## CLUES

1. Andrews lost the least amount on a sport that stresses a man's speed. His bet was made three months after another person bet on the horse race.

2. Gonzales made his bet in one of the coldest months of the year.

3. Jameson lost his bet on an event that pits two men against each other.

4. Henrickson lost $2 less than the person who lost the most and $2 more than the person who lost the least. He bet on a sport that would eventually evolve into the sport known as baseball.

5. The person who bet in January lost the most.

6. The person who bet on a man's sense of balance lost $4 in May.

7. Jameson lost twice as much as Andrews in a month that is the shortest of the year.

8. Henrickson's bet was made one month before the man who lost the least.

9. Lymenstall owned a sawmill, and the only sports he was interested in were the ones involving his industry.

Name: _____ Date: _____

# Sports Logic Problem Solution Chart

|  | Rounders | Log Rolling | Horse Racing | Foot Racing | Wrestling | January | February | March | April | May | One Dollar | Two Dollars | Three Dollars | Four Dollars | Five Dollars |
|---|---|---|---|---|---|---|---|---|---|---|---|---|---|---|---|
| **Andrews** |  |  |  |  |  |  |  |  |  |  |  |  |  |  |  |
| **Jameson** |  |  |  |  |  |  |  |  |  |  |  |  |  |  |  |
| **Gonzales** |  |  |  |  |  |  |  |  |  |  |  |  |  |  |  |
| **Henrickson** |  |  |  |  |  |  |  |  |  |  |  |  |  |  |  |
| **Lymenstall** |  |  |  |  |  |  |  |  |  |  |  |  |  |  |  |
| **One Dollar** |  |  |  |  |  |  |  |  |  |  |  |  |  |  |  |
| **Two Dollars** |  |  |  |  |  |  |  |  |  |  |  |  |  |  |  |
| **Three Dollars** |  |  |  |  |  |  |  |  |  |  |  |  |  |  |  |
| **Four Dollars** |  |  |  |  |  |  |  |  |  |  |  |  |  |  |  |
| **Five Dollars** |  |  |  |  |  |  |  |  |  |  |  |  |  |  |  |
| **January** |  |  |  |  |  |  |  |  |  |  |  |  |  |  |  |
| **February** |  |  |  |  |  |  |  |  |  |  |  |  |  |  |  |
| **March** |  |  |  |  |  |  |  |  |  |  |  |  |  |  |  |
| **April** |  |  |  |  |  |  |  |  |  |  |  |  |  |  |  |
| **May** |  |  |  |  |  |  |  |  |  |  |  |  |  |  |  |

| Name | Event | Month | Money Lost |
|---|---|---|---|
| Andrews |  |  |  |
| Jameson |  |  |  |
| Gonzales |  |  |  |
| Henrickson |  |  |  |
| Lymenstall |  |  |  |

Name: _____ Date: _____

# The Colonies
## CRIME AND PUNISHMENT

Crime and punishment in the colonies were much different from region to region, as well as from period to period. First offenders were often treated leniently, but repeat offenders could receive a death sentence. While many offenses that we would consider minor today had very serious penalties, it is not clear how strictly and consistently these laws were enforced. For example, since the colonies needed men to work, hunt, and farm, it is not likely they would execute someone for a relatively minor violation.

For the most part, those found guilty of some crime were not sent to prison. This was considered a waste of taxpayers' money. Both corporal (physical) and capital (death) sentences were common.

Given below are strange and unusual facts concerning crime and punishment during the colonial period. Read each of the following sentences and circle the letter before the correct answer.

1.  The Puritans forbade:
    A. Singing of Christmas carols.          B. Trade with the Indians.
    C. Salad bars.                           D. Eating meat on Sunday.

2.  In colonial times, someone who swore could be fined and:
    A. Banished.                             B. Have his mouth washed with soap.
    C. Whipped.                              D. Set in a corner.

3.  If a child broke the law in the colonies:
    A. He received a slap on the wrist.      B. The father could be punished.
    C. He was ignored.                       D. He would have to wear a dunce hat.

4.   In the latter part of the 17th century in New England, it was a crime to:
    A. Dress too elegantly.                  B. Whistle after dark.
    C. Beat your horse.                      D. Spank your children.

5.  When two boys were talking in class, they would often be:
    A. Made to wear a fake donkey's head.    B. Joined and sticks were put in their mouths.
    C. Made to wear a dress.                 D. Sent home.

6.  The punishment for a woman found guilty of emptying dirty water in the streets was:
    A. Cleaning the streets.                 B. Community service.
    C. Shearing her hair.                    D. Receiving the lash.

Name: _____ Date: _____

7.  Complaining out loud could result in a man:
    A. Not being permitted to talk for a week.    B. Having ice poured down his sleeve.
    C. Confessing his sin in church.              D. Having his tongue cut out.

8.  Naughty school children were:
    A. Whipped with willow rods.                  B. Forced to sit on tacks.
    C. Forced to clean blackboards.               D. Forced to cut wood for the fireplace.

9.  A woman who committed crimes might be released and:
    A. Be required to do community service.       B. Be required to serve the church.
    C. Banished from the colony.                  D. Her husband sentenced.

10.  When someone was convicted of a crime and not executed, they would sometimes be:
    A. Branded on the hand.                       B. Given house arrest.
    C. Stripped of their worldly possessions.     D. Excommunicated.

11.  Other punishments in colonial times were stocks, which were a pair of boards with holes for
    the ankles and a sharpened edge of a board for the seat, and the pillory, which was a board
    with holes for the head and hands. People would throw rotten fruit, eggs, and all sorts of
    garbage at them. Someone who received this punishment would be wise to hire someone
    to wipe his or her face from time to time so that he or she:
    A. Wouldn't get sweat in his or her eyes.     B. Wouldn't get sick.
    C. Wouldn't suffocate.                        D. Would feel more comfortable.

12.  In 1658 Virginia passed a law expelling all _____ from the colony.
    A. Money lenders                              B. Attorneys
    C. Undertakers                                D. Wine makers

# The Colonies: Crime and Punishment—Answer Sheet

1. **A.**  **Singing of Christmas carols.**
2. **C.**  **Whipped.**
3. **B.**  **The father could be punished.**
4. **A.**  **Dress too elegantly.** Thirty men were arrested in 1675 in New England for wearing clothes that were considered above their station. Thirty-eight women were also arrested for the same offense in Connecticut.
5. **B.**  **Joined and sticks were put in their mouths.** This was called "yoking." The boys were joined together and two "whispering sticks" were put into their mouths. Whispering sticks were small bits of wood. At other times they might be made to sit on a one-legged stool, wear a birch rod in their collars, wear a dunce hat, or wear signs that said "Idle Boy" or "Telltale."
6. **D.**  **Receiving the lash.**
7. **B.**  **Having ice poured down his sleeve.**
8. **A.**  **Whipped with willow rods.**
9. **D.**  **Her husband sentenced.** A husband was usually liable for his wife's crimes, unless he could prove that he was not present or should not be blamed. A woman who committed crimes might be released and her husband sentenced, or they both might be sentenced.
10. **A.**  **Branded on the hand.** This punishment was called: "Burned at the Hand." It was a branding on the base of the thumb of the right hand. From this punishment comes the custom of raising one's hand when swearing in court. The court could see if a person had been found guilty of previous crimes.
11. **C.**  **They wouldn't suffocate.** While you could argue that any of these answers would be correct, the *main* reason someone was needed to wipe the person's face was so that

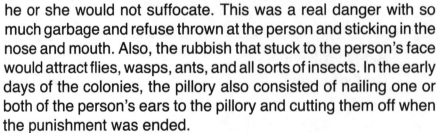

he or she would not suffocate. This was a real danger with so much garbage and refuse thrown at the person and sticking in the nose and mouth. Also, the rubbish that stuck to the person's face would attract flies, wasps, ants, and all sorts of insects. In the early days of the colonies, the pillory also consisted of nailing one or both of the person's ears to the pillory and cutting them off when the punishment was ended.

12. **B.**  **Attorneys.** Disdain for lawyers was so widespread that in 1641, Massachusetts Bay Colony passed a law making it illegal to earn money by representing a person in court. Both the Virginia and the Massachusetts laws stayed on the books for several years before they were repealed.

Name: _____ Date: _____

# Make a Whirligig

Colonial children did not have the large number or the variety of toys that are available today. When the settlers sailed from their homeland to America, there was no room for toys. All of the available space was used for food, clothing, tools, and other items necessary for survival in the primitive new world. Once here, there was no money to buy toys, so children needed to make their own toys from whatever materials they could find. One of the most common toys, and the easiest to make, was a whirligig. Below are the directions for making this simple and enjoyable toy.

**Materials Needed**: Cardboard, lid of a jar or a compass, string, pencil

**Procedure**:

• Draw a circle about 3 inches in diameter on the heavy cardboard. You can make the circle with a compass, or by tracing around the lid of a jar with a pencil. (You might want to experiment with different sizes of circles. Some students in class can make larger ones, and some can make smaller ones.)

• Cut out the circle and color it. Try different patterns and colors. Spiral designs work particularly well.

• Punch two small, diagonal holes in the circle, each about $\frac{3}{8}$-inch from the center of the circle.

• Thread about 3 feet of string through the holes and tie the ends together. (If your circle was larger than 3 inches, you can try a longer string. If it was less than three inches, your string should be shorter.)

**Using the Whirligig**: Holding the string with the index finger and the thumb of each hand, twirl the circle until the string is tight. Stretch the string out and pull it hard to make the whirligig spin, then relax as the whirligig spins and rewinds. When the string is tight again, pull hard. Continue the routine of pulling and relaxing and enjoy the colored patterns you have drawn on your whirligig.

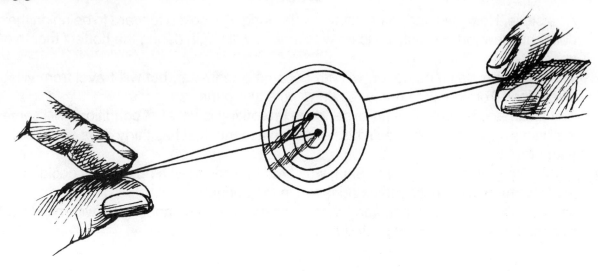

Name: _____ Date: _____

# Releasing Slaves Logic Problem

Randolph Townsend was a wealthy tobacco farmer in South Carolina who lived an easy life; however, he was unhappy and felt there was something missing in his life. One day a traveling preacher, missionary, and abolitionist passed by Townsend's plantation, and Townsend invited him in for supper and asked him to stay the night. An abolitionist was someone who wanted to abolish slavery. After talking with the preacher about life, religion, freedom, and slavery until dawn, Townsend invited the man to stay on for several weeks. Over that time Townsend came to realize the evils of slavery and decided to free the slaves he had working on his plantation. He knew that once they were free, they would need to get jobs to support themselves and their families. The kind of jobs they did on the plantation might not be available or would pay too little. So rather than free all of the slaves at the same time, he decided to train them for new jobs and release them over a several-month period as each became trained in his field. The first slave would be released in January.

The names of the slaves were James, Thomas, Seth, Andrew, and Henry. Their jobs as slaves, in no particular order, were field hand, horse groomer, butler, gardener, and coachman. The new jobs for which they were being trained, again in no particular order, would be farmer, blacksmith, cooper, teamster, and tinker.

Each slave's name is shown in the box on the next page. From the clues given below, figure out what each man's job is now, the new job he will have when he is freed, and the month he will attain his freedom.

Solving a logic problem is fun but challenging. All the information you need to solve this problem is given either in the introduction or in the clues. In addition to using the clues, you must also use logic to solve the problem. In order to solve the problem, you may use the solution chart on the next page. Write "yes" in the appropriate box on the chart when you discover a correct answer and "no" when you are sure that the box represents an incorrect answer. Sometimes as you work through the problem and fill out the solution chart, you may get stumped and need to guess at an answer. If you do guess, you can test the guess to see if it would work out with the clues you were given. If you discover your guess is incorrect, you can always change it on the solution chart.

## CLUES

1. As a slave, Henry worked in the house all day long. He looked forward to being on the road doing his new job. His only concern was that he will begin during the hottest month of the year.
2. Thomas, who was a gardener, will not become a teamster, but will travel from village to village and from home to home repairing pots and pans.
3. The field hand realizes that his experience in working in very hot conditions will serve him well in his new job. He will begin his new job in a month that has thirty days and is noted for a lot of rain.
4. The horse groomer, who is not Seth, was tired of working with horses but decided to stay in agriculture. He is happy to be released in the spring.
5. James, who is now a coachman, will be working with his hands for a winery. He will be released in a month that has thirty-one days.

Name:_____ Date:_____

# Releasing Slaves Solution Chart

|  | Field Hand | Horse Groomer | Butler | Gardener | Coachman | January | February | April | June | August | Farmer | Blacksmith | Cooper | Teamster | Tinker |
|---|---|---|---|---|---|---|---|---|---|---|---|---|---|---|---|
| **James** |  |  |  |  |  |  |  |  |  |  |  |  |  |  |  |
| **Thomas** |  |  |  |  |  |  |  |  |  |  |  |  |  |  |  |  |
| **Seth** |  |  |  |  |  |  |  |  |  |  |  |  |  |  |  |  |
| **Andrew** |  |  |  |  |  |  |  |  |  |  |  |  |  |  |  |  |
| **Henry** |  |  |  |  |  |  |  |  |  |  |  |  |  |  |  |  |
| **January** |  |  |  |  |  |  |  |  |  |  |  |  |  |  |  |  |
| **February** |  |  |  |  |  |  |  |  |  |  |  |  |  |  |  |  |
| **April** |  |  |  |  |  |  |  |  |  |  |  |  |  |  |  |  |
| **June** |  |  |  |  |  |  |  |  |  |  |  |  |  |  |  |  |
| **August** |  |  |  |  |  |  |  |  |  |  |  |  |  |  |  |  |
| **Farmer** |  |  |  |  |  |  |  |  |  |  |  |  |  |  |  |  |
| **Blacksmith** |  |  |  |  |  |  |  |  |  |  |  |  |  |  |  |  |
| **Cooper** |  |  |  |  |  |  |  |  |  |  |  |  |  |  |  |  |
| **Teamster** |  |  |  |  |  |  |  |  |  |  |  |  |  |  |  |  |
| **Tinker** |  |  |  |  |  |  |  |  |  |  |  |  |  |  |  |  |

| Name | Job as Slave | Job as Freeman | Month |
|---|---|---|---|
| James |  |  |  |
| Thomas |  |  |  |
| Seth |  |  |  |
| Andrew |  |  |  |
| Henry |  |  |  |

33

Name: _____ Date: _____

# The Colonies
## RELIGION

We tend to think of the colonists as very religious people. Certainly, religion played an important part in the lives of these people. It should be remembered, however, that the emphasis on religion varied among the colonies, and it was not the same throughout all of the periods the colonies were in existence. Religion was more important during the early periods of the colonies. When a person is starving or afraid of being attacked by an Indian or killed by a bear, faith in God is a natural reaction. In fact, in some early colonies, the mortality rates ran as high as 75 percent. When life becomes easier and there is not as much danger, religion sometimes receives less attention.

As you will see from the following quiz, when a person in the village did not meet his or her religious obligations, there was often a very severe punishment. Again, these punishments varied from region to region and from period to period. Also, there are few records to indicate how often these harsh punishments were actually carried out.

Given below are strange and unusual facts concerning religion during the colonial period. Read each of the following sentences and circle the letter before the correct answer.

1. Dogs were permitted to attend the church services in early New England in order to:
   A. Provide amusement for the children.    B. Keep the congregation awake.
   C. Catch mice and rats.                   D. Keep their masters' feet warm.

2. Seats in Puritan churches were assigned according to:
   A. Rank and wealth.                       B. Sex.
   C. Length of membership.                  D. Height.

3. In 1660, Mary Dyer, a mother of seven, was hanged in Boston because:
   A. She was accused of witchcraft.         B. She was a Quaker.
   C. She brewed beer.                       D. She married an Indian.

4. Disagreeing or questioning a minister could result in being:
   A. Publicly criticized.                   B. Put into stocks.
   C. Put to death.                          D. Put into bonds.

5. Quakers had no:
   A. Donations in currency.                 B. Strong feelings about religion.
   C. Church or meeting house.               D. Ministers or sermons.

6. Puritans felt this day was more important than Christmas.
   A. Labor Day                              B. Easter
   C. Independence Day                       D. Arbor Day

Name: _____ Date: _____

7. The Quakers and Indians got along well together; in fact, Indians often:
   A. Invited Quakers to feasts.              B. Attended Quaker meetings.
   C. Baby-sat for the Quakers.               D. Protected the Quakers.

8. Quakers felt that their religion was so much better than others, that they would:
   A. Interrupt services of other churches.   B. Try to convert everyone they met.
   C. Only speak to Quakers.                  D. Only do business with Quakers.

9. In 1644, Massachusetts would banish anyone who refused to have their child:
   A. Serve in church.                        B. Baptized.
   C. Attend school.                          D. Potty-trained.

10. In the early colonial period, churches had a person called a tithing man. If a tithing man saw a man going to sleep during the service, his job was to:
    A. Get him a pillow.                       B. Stick him with a pin.
    C. Hit him in the head with a pole.        D. Escort him out of church.

11. A person who preached falsely or spoke against the religion was sometimes punished by putting:
    A. Him or her in a cage in church.         B. Him or her in a cart and parading them.
    C. A devil's costume on him or her.        D. A hot awl through his or her tongue.

12. New Englanders thought most forms of pleasure:
    A. Were overrated.                         B. Were sinful and wicked.
    C. Should be taken in moderation.          D. Were few and far between.

13. In Puritan New England, people who celebrated Christmas:
    A. Did so on December 25.                  B. Did so on the first day of spring.
    C. Did so whenever the village decided.    D. Were punished.

14. In Puritan New England, it was a crime for ministers to:
    A. Wear a cross made of brass.             B. Perform wedding ceremonies.
    C. Ride a horse on Sunday.                 D. Work with their hands.

15. In Virginia, missing church once on Sunday resulted in the loss of rations for a week. Missing church two times on Sunday meant the loss of rations as well as suffering a whipping. Missing church three times on Sunday meant the person was:
    A. Excommunicated.                         B. Put to death.
    C. Banished.                               D. Deprived of his attendance pin.

35

# The Colonies: Religion—Answer Sheet

1. **D.** **Keep their masters' feet warm.** The churches were not heated, so dogs were permitted to attend the service so they could sleep on their masters' feet and keep them warm. Women and children used foot stoves. These were metal boxes that had hot coals or heated bricks in them to keep their feet warm.

2. **A.** **Rank and wealth.** Older, wealthy members got the best seats—the ones closest to the front. If anyone sat in a seat that was not assigned to him, he was removed and fined.

3. **B.** **She was a Quaker.** Quakers were persecuted in New England. They paid fines, were whipped, thrown in prison, and even hanged. Mary had been exiled from Boston twice. When she learned that two Quakers were to be executed for refusing to leave Boston, she went to join them. The three were tried, found guilty, and ordered to leave the colony. They refused and were hanged.

4. **C.** **Put to death.** Disagreeing or questioning a minister was considered heresy.

5. **D.** **Ministers or sermons.** Quakers would enter church and sit quietly. If someone felt he was moved by God to speak, he would rise and speak. If no one was moved to speak, they just sat in silence until it was time to leave.

6. **B.** **Easter.** Easter celebrated the death and resurrection of Jesus as well as the salvation of humans and so was more important to Puritans than Jesus's birth.

7. **C.** **Baby-sat for the Quakers.** The Quakers told the Indians they did not believe in fighting, and they would never fight with them. The Indians also said they wanted peace. Both parties kept their word. The Quakers visited the Indian camps and never brought weapons. The Indians gave the Quakers food in the winter. If the Quakers had to go on a trip, the Indians looked after their children.

8. **A.** **Interrupt services of other churches.**

9. **B.** **Baptized.**

10. **C.** **Hit him in the head with a pole.** The tithing man's main job was to watch people during the service. He would quiet down noisy children. If he saw a woman starting to fall asleep, he would touch her face with a long pole that had a fox tail on the end. But if he saw a man about to sleep, he would give him a sharp blow on top of the head with the wooden end of the pole.

11. **D.** **A hot awl through his or her tongue.**

12. **B.** **Were sinful and wicked.**

13. **D.** **Were punished. It was illegal to observe Christmas.** In 1659, the Puritans repealed a law that said observing Christmas by not working, feasting, or in any other way was prohibited, but the holiday still was not observed. It was considered just another workday. It wasn't until the middle of the nineteenth century that Christmas became a major holiday.

14. **B.** **Perform wedding ceremonies.** The New England Puritans felt that marriage was a worldly, not a religious, matter and had nothing to do with the church. Traditionally, marriage was needed so that there could be legal heirs. In this way, money, property, and in some cases a title could be passed on to the next generation. Near the end of the seventeenth century, the church relaxed its rules, and marriages became common in churches.

15. **B.** **Put to death.**

Name: _____ Date: _____

# Buying Horses Logic Problem

During the glacial periods, the prehistoric ancestors of the modern horse became extinct in North America. It was not until the Spaniards came to this continent after Columbus's exploration that horses were reintroduced into the New World. The horse had an important effect on many Native American cultures. Indians became more effective hunters and warriors.

Horses were very important in the early American colonies as well. Horses were used for transportation, work, and power on the farm and for recreation. Nearly everyone had some contact with horses.

Periodically in the colonies there would be a horse sale. Those who had horses to sell or trade would bring them to a sale lot, and those who wished to buy would arrive and inspect the horses. There was haggling, bargaining, and joking as each man tried to make the best deal possible. Horse trading was a social event as well as a business transaction. Horse trading was a skill that was admired and envied.

The selling of horses provides a basis for our brain-numbing logic problem. At a horse sale, five friends, whose names were Mr. Lewis, Mr. Carver, Mr. Holmes, Mr. Ogle, and Mr. San Martin, each bought a different kind of horse. Each horse was purchased with a specific purpose in mind. One horse was bought to plow fields, another was bought for racing, and so on. Unfortunately, shortly after the sale, each horse died or became disabled from a different disease or accident. From the clues given below, can you figure out who bought which horse, for what purpose the horse was purchased, and how the horse died?

Solving a logic problem is fun but challenging. All the information you need to solve this problem is given either in the introduction or in the clues. In addition to using the clues, you must also use logic to solve the problem. In order to solve the problem, you may use the solution chart on the next page. Write "yes" in the appropriate box on the chart when you discover a correct answer and "no" when you are sure that the box represents an incorrect answer. Sometimes, as you work through the problem and fill out the solution chart, you may get stumped and need to guess at an answer. If you do guess, you can test your guess to see if it would work out with the clues you were given. If you discover your guess is incorrect, you can always change it on the solution chart.

## CLUES

1. Mr. Holmes' horse broke its leg.
2. Mr. Lewis bought the spotted horse. It was not the horse purchased for racing.
3. The chestnut horse was not bought to pull wagons.
4. Mr. Holmes gave the horse he bought to his daughter on her birthday. She loved its golden coat and cream-colored mane and tail. It did not die of any disease.
5. Mr. San Martin's horse, which was not chestnut, was retired from racing after a problem with its leg.
6. Mr. Carver had hoped that the white horse he bought could be used to produce other fine horses for his farm. Unfortunately it died, apparently after eating something.
7. An accident while plowing the field apparently caused the infectious disease that killed the chestnut horse.

Name: _____ Date: _____

# Buying Horses Solution Chart

|  | Black | White | Spotted | Palomino | Chestnut | Plowing | Racing | Breeding | Pulling Wagons | Recreational Riding | Botulism | Tetanus | Broken Leg | Blindness | Lame |
|---|---|---|---|---|---|---|---|---|---|---|---|---|---|---|---|
| Mr. Lewis |  |  |  |  |  |  |  |  |  |  |  |  |  |  |  |
| Mr. Carver |  |  |  |  |  |  |  |  |  |  |  |  |  |  |  |
| Mr. Holmes |  |  |  |  |  |  |  |  |  |  |  |  |  |  |  |
| Mr. Ogle |  |  |  |  |  |  |  |  |  |  |  |  |  |  |  |
| Mr. San Martin |  |  |  |  |  |  |  |  |  |  |  |  |  |  |  |
| Botulism |  |  |  |  |  |  |  |  |  |  |  |  |  |  |  |
| Tetanus |  |  |  |  |  |  |  |  |  |  |  |  |  |  |  |
| Broken Leg |  |  |  |  |  |  |  |  |  |  |  |  |  |  |  |
| Blindness |  |  |  |  |  |  |  |  |  |  |  |  |  |  |  |
| Lame |  |  |  |  |  |  |  |  |  |  |  |  |  |  |  |
| Plowing |  |  |  |  |  |  |  |  |  |  |  |  |  |  |  |
| Racing |  |  |  |  |  |  |  |  |  |  |  |  |  |  |  |
| Breeding |  |  |  |  |  |  |  |  |  |  |  |  |  |  |  |
| Pulling Wagons |  |  |  |  |  |  |  |  |  |  |  |  |  |  |  |
| Recreational Riding |  |  |  |  |  |  |  |  |  |  |  |  |  |  |  |

| Name | Color of Horse | Reason for Buying | Disease/Injury |
|---|---|---|---|
| Lewis |  |  |  |
| Carver |  |  |  |
| Holmes |  |  |  |
| Ogle |  |  |  |
| San Martin |  |  |  |

Name: _____ Date: _____

# Declaration of Independence

It is not an exaggeration to say that the Declaration of Independence, written by Thomas Jefferson, is one of the most inspiring and honored documents in U.S. history. When it was adopted by the Continental Congress, it marked the birth of a new nation. Congress had appointed a "committee of five" to draft a statement to the world presenting the colonies' case for independence. The committee consisted of John Adams, Benjamin Franklin, Thomas Jefferson, Robert R. Livingston, and Roger Sherman. Jefferson was given the task of writing the original document. After a few changes were made, the document was submitted to Congress. Two passages in the draft were rejected by the Congress. But, for the most part, the Declaration was adopted as Jefferson had written it, without major change.

Given below are strange and unusual facts concerning the Declaration of Independence. Read each of the following sentences and circle the letter before the correct answer.

1. What happened on July 4, 1776?
   A. Declaration of Independence signed
   C. Declaration of Independence written
   B. Declaration of Independence adopted
   D. Independence Day sales

2. Tradition says that John Hancock wrote his name large so that:
   A. He could see it without his glasses.
   C. King George could read it.
   B. To make him feel important.
   D. It could be used to sell insurance.

3. Who wrote the first Declaration of Independence for the colonies?
   A. Thomas Jefferson
   C. Squanto
   B. James Madison
   D. Benjamin Franklin

4. The Declaration of Independence, as first written by Thomas Jefferson, included a clause abolishing:
   A. Mandatory church attendance.
   C. The Department of Education.
   B. Use of tobacco in federal buildings.
   D. Slavery.

Name: _____  Date: _____

5.  We all know that the Declaration of Independence states that our "inalienable rights" include, "life, liberty and the pursuit of happiness." In an earlier draft of the document however, the phrase originally read: "life, liberty and the pursuit of _____.
    A. Property                              B. Pleasure
    C. The opposite sex                      D. Excellence

6.  There was only one person who signed the following four documents: Articles of Association, the Declaration of Independence, the Articles of Confederation, and the U.S. Constitution. That person was:
    A. Thomas Jefferson.                     B. John Adams.
    C. Roger Sherman.                        D. George Jefferson.

7.  Only one person recanted (took back, withdrew, changed his mind about) his signing of the Declaration of Independence. He was:
    A. Richard Stockton.                     B. Roger Sherman.
    C. John Hancock.                         D. Benedict Arnold.

8.  Two patriots died within hours of each another on July 4, 1826, which was the fiftieth anniversary of Independence Day. They were:
    A. Hamilton and Washington.              B. Adams and Jefferson.
    C. Burns and Allen.                      D. Burr and Franklin.

9.  On July 4, 1776, the Liberty Bell:
    A. Rang.                                 B. Did not ring.
    C. Was in for repair.                    D. Had not yet been made.

10. The Declaration of Independence begins with what words?
    A. We the people of the United States... B. When in the course of human events...
    C. Four score and seven years ago...     D. Friends, Americans, countrymen...

11. Who was originally considered for the task of writing the Declaration of Independence?
    A. Thomas Jefferson                      B. Patrick Henry
    C. Richard Henry Lee                     D. Richard Kimball

# Declaration of Independence—Answer Sheet

1.  **B.**  **Declaration of Independence adopted.** Although the Declaration of Independence was dated July 4th, 1776, Independence was actually declared two days earlier on July 2nd. The final draft approving the Declaration of Independence occurred on July 4th. The document was not signed on the fourth although John Hancock and the Congressional secretary, Charles Thomson, did sign one copy of the Declaration on that day. The official ceremony and signing took place on August 2, 1776. Six members signed later. One did not sign until 1781.

2.  **C.**  **King George could read it.** Legend has it that John Hancock wrote his name large so King George could read it. However, there is no proof that this story true.

3.  **D.**  **Benjamin Franklin.** Thomas Jefferson was enthusiastic about the document Franklin wrote but observed that other delegates at the Continental Congress found it upsetting. About a year later, Jefferson wrote what we now know as the Declaration of Independence, and Congress approved it.

4.  **D.**  **Slavery.** Jefferson included a clause abolishing slavery in the original draft, but under pressure from the other delegates, deleted it.

5.  **A.**  **Property.**

6.  **C.**  **Roger Sherman.**

7.  **A.**  **Richard Stockton.**

8.  **B.**  **Adams and Jefferson.** In a strange twist of fate, the two men who had worked so hard together to produce the Declaration of Independence, and the only two who had signed the document and gone on to become Presidents of the United States, died within hours of each other. Stranger still, they both died on July 4, 1826, the fiftieth anniversary of the signing of the historical document.

9.  **B.**  **Did not ring.** Legend says just the opposite. While the Liberty Bell did hang in the statehouse in Philadelphia in 1776, it had lost significance. In 1828, the city of Philadelphia tried to sell the bell for scrap, but no one would buy it. It wasn't worth the trouble or expense to remove it.

10. **B.**  **When in the course of human events...**

11. **C.**  **Richard Henry Lee.** He made a resolution that said, "these United Colonies are, and of right ought to be, free and independent States." The resolution was approved by the Continental Congress July 2, 1776. According to parliamentary procedure, Lee would have been appointed chairman of the committee to furnish the Declaration of Independence. However, on the day his resolution was approved, Lee was unexpectedly summoned home to Virginia because some members of his family were ill. Since Lee was not available, Thomas Jefferson was elected to write the Declaration.

Name: _____ Date: _____

# Revolutionary War
## GENERAL FACTS

As a result of the American Revolution, which was the war between the American colonists and England, the United States of America was created. America was among the first countries to put into practice many ideas and theories that had often been talked about, but seldom practiced. Some of these ideas were the separation of church and state, government of the people, and a system of checks and balances in government. However, much of what we have learned in school about the American Revolution is simply not true; there are other facts that have not been discussed widely.

Read each of the following sentences and circle the letter before the correct answer.

1. The Boston Massacre began when some young male colonists:
   A. Attacked a British sentry.          B. Threw snowballs at a British sentry.
   C. Burned a British flag.              D. Burned a picture of King George.

2. The song "Yankee Doodle" was originally:
   A. A French and Indian War song.       B. A Revolutionary War song.
   C. A nursery rhyme.                     D. An advertising jingle.

3. The lyrics of the song "Yankee Doodle" were meant to ridicule:
   A. American bravery.                    B. English cowardice.
   C. The uniforms of the colonists.       D. An American general.

4. The Boston Tea Party was a result of a British tax on tea. With the new tax, tea in America cost:
   A. Less than it did in England.         B. The same as it did in England.
   C. Twice as much as it did in England.  D. Ten times as much as it did in England.

5. What do the following cities have in common: Philadelphia, York, Lancaster, Baltimore, Annapolis, Princeton, Trenton, and New York City?
   A. Site of major battles in Revolution  B. Sites of tea parties
   C. All on Paul Revere's route           D. Served as the seat of government

6. This city was second only to London as the largest English-speaking city in the world at the time of the War of Independence.
   A. Boston                               B. Quebec
   C. New York                             D. Philadelphia

Name: _____ Date: _____

7.  The original thirteen colonies, as well as the Revolutionary War, were financed with the help of:

    A. Lotteries.                              B. Graduated income taxes.
    C. Value added taxes.                      D. Thumb taxes.

8.  During the American Revolution, many brides wore:

    A. Red, white, and blue gowns.             B. Blue and white gowns.
    C. Red gowns.                              D. Colonist army coats.

9.  Betsy Ross's important contribution to the American Revolution was:

    A. Designing the first American flag.      B. Selling war bonds.
    C. Running a munitions factory.            D. Giving USO shows.

10. How many Boston Tea Parties were there?

    A. None                                    B. One
    C. Two                                     D. Three

11. Emmanuel Leutze was hired to paint a mural of George Washington crossing the Delaware River on December 12, 1776. He used the _____ as a model for the Delaware.

    A. Mississippi                             B. Potomac
    C. Rhine                                   D. Moon River

12. The tax imposed on tea that was the cause of the Boston Tea Party in 1773 was:

    A. One cent per pound.                     B. Three cents per pound.
    C. Ten cents per pound.                    D. Twenty-five cents per pound.

13. The Americans lost the Battle of Bunker Hill when:

    A. Their Drum and Fife Corps retreated.    B. The Minutemen were a minute late.
    C. The colonists did not fight well.       D. They ran out of gunpowder.

14. What is the name of the oldest commissioned U.S. naval vessel?

    A. *The Monitor*                           B. *The Merrimack*
    C. *The John Paul Jones*                   D. *The Constitution*

15. In New York Harbor in 1776, something occurred that changed the navy. What?

    A. History's first submarine attack        B. A naval attack using surfboards
    C. The first diesel-powered ship           D. A machine gunboat

# Revolutionary War: General Facts—Answer Sheet

1. **B.** **Threw snowballs at a British sentry.** Five Americans were killed. The first one killed was a former slave named Crispus Attucks. The race of Attucks is unclear. Some say he was black, some say he was an Indian or a combination of both.

2. **A.** **French and Indian War song.**

3. **C.** **The uniforms of the colonists.** The term "doodle" in colonial times meant one who was stupid. "Macaroni" meant a fancy dresser. At the Battle of Concord, the British troops marched into battle playing "Yankee Doodle." When they retreated from the Americans, the Americans' fife and drums began playing the song. From that point on, it became an American tune.

4. **A.** **Less than it did in England.**

5. **D.** **Served as the seat of government.** All of these cities served as the seat of government for the United States of America before Washington, D.C., became the nation's capital.

6. **D.** **Philadelphia.**

7. **A.** **Lotteries.** Lotteries are not new. Not only were the original thirteen colonies and Revolutionary War financed with the help of lotteries, so was the Civil War.

8. **C.** **Red gowns.** During the American Revolution, many brides chose not to wear white gowns, but red gowns as a symbol of rebellion.

9. **C.** **Running a munitions factory.** Betsy Ross ran a munitions factory from her basement.

10. **C.** **Two.** The more famous "Tea Party" occurred when between 50 and 60 "Sons of Liberty" disguised themselves as Mohawks and protested the three cents per pound British tax on tea by dumping chests of tea into Boston Harbor. Not so well known is that Bostonians repeated the performance on March 7, 1774. In addition, there were copycat tea parties in other states. One of the tea parties in Maryland was known as the Peggy Stewart Tea Party—named after the tea ship burned by the colonists.

11. **C.** **Rhine.** He used the Rhine as a model for the Delaware, and the flag he painted was not adopted until 1777, a year after the 1776 crossing.

12. **B.** **Three cents per pound.**

13. **D.** **They ran out of gunpowder.** As a result, they were forced to retreat.

14. **D.** **The Constitution.**

15. **A.** **History's first submarine attack.** David Bushnell, a Connecticut inventor, called his submarine the *Turtle* because it looked like two large turtle shells joined together. The watertight vessel was made of 6-inch-thick oak timbers coated with tar. On September 6, 1776, the *Turtle* attempted to sink the *HMS Eagle*, flagship of the British fleet. The plan was for the submarine to secure a cask of gunpowder to the hull of the *Eagle* and sneak away before it exploded. It didn't work that way. The *Turtle* got tangled up with the *Eagle*'s rudder bar, lost ballast, and surfaced before the gunpowder could be planted.

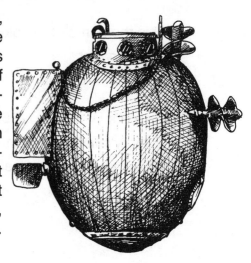

Name: _____ Date: _____

# Revolutionary War
## PEOPLE

Unlike many other wars, when we think about the Revolutionary War, we think less about the battles and dates and more about the people involved. George Washington, Patrick Henry, Paul Revere, and a host of other patriotic colonists leap to mind at the thought of the American Revolution. Of course, it isn't just the colonist leaders whom we remember. The vision of a minuteman leaving his plow in the field as he grabs his rifle is one that every American has etched in his or her mind. These soldiers sometimes did not have powder for their rifles or shoes to wear, but they fought bravely. Fighting on their own land, sometimes in small groups, the Continental Army caused heavy casualties to the English, who found it difficult to get replacements. Colonists, on the other hand, usually were able to get men to fight. Sometimes they even used English deserters, slaves, and criminals.

Shown below are some strange and little-known facts about the American Revolution and the people who fought in the war. As you read the answers, you will probably be surprised that many of the things you read about this conflict are either not true or there is no evidence to prove that they really happened. Read each of the following sentences and circle the letter before the correct answer.

1. Patrick Henry was a member of the Virginia legislature after the Revolutionary War. He supported taxes that were _____ that which would have been imposed by the Stamp Act.

   A. Much lower than                    B. Much greater than
   C. Identical to                       D. Easier to pay than

2. Benjamin Franklin was once considered:

   A. The uncle of his country.          B. A traitor.
   C. President Pro Tem.                 D. A member of the Cherokee tribe.

3. In 1775, Franklin was angry with the British over their treatment of the colonies and was disgusted by the fighting at Lexington and Concord, so he:

   A. Gave a speech at Independence Hall.   B. Wrote King George.
   C. Wrote a Declaration of Independence.  D. Struck an English officer.

4. Who warned the American colonists that the British were coming?

   A. Paul Revere                        B. William Dawes and Samuel Prescott
   C. Revere, Dawes, and Prescott        D. Nostradamus

5. Many people considered Paul Revere to be the greatest silversmith of colonial America. However, he was a failure at his second trade, which was:

   A. Copperplate engraving.             B. Candlestick maker.
   C. Master jeweler.                    D. Owner of a "Big and Tall" shop for men.

Name: _____ Date: _____

6.  During his midnight ride on April 18, 1775, Paul Revere shouted:
    A. "The British are coming."          B. "The regulars are coming."
    C. "Our adversary has arrived via ship."   D. "Here come the Redcoats."

7.  What many consider unusual about the Constitutional Convention of 1787 was that Thomas Jefferson, John Adams, Samuel Adams, and Patrick Henry:
    A. Did not give speeches.              B. Did not speak to each other.
    C. Did not attend.                     D. Each spoke for more than two hours.

8.  Patrick Henry said, "I would rather have a _____ than the new government."
    A. King                                B. Good cigar
    C. Good horse                          D. Better government

9.  John Adams defended _____ after the _____.
    A. Colonists, Boston Tea Party         B. Loyalists, Bunker Hill
    C. British soldiers, Boston Massacre   D. Circus owners, Stamp Act

10. Patrick Henry was a lawyer who once defended a group of farmers because they paid their clergymen in:
    A. Tobacco.                            B. Cash.
    C. English pounds.                     D. Pigs.

11. Who was the first President of the United States?
    A. George Washington                   B. Benjamin Franklin
    C. John Hanson                         D. John Smith

12. Why was Mary Ludwig Hays (later McCauley) called Molly Pitcher?
    A. She had very large ears.            B. She carried water in a pitcher to soldiers.
    C. She was a pitcher on a softball team.   D. She was a champion horseshoe pitcher.

13. Who designed America's first flag?
    A. Betsy Ross                          B. Molly Pitcher
    C. Fannie Flag                         D. Unknown

14. During the American Revolution, General Rahl, commander of the Hessian mercenaries fighting for the British, received a note from a spy that said George Washington was about to cross the Delaware and launch an attack. The general was so immersed in _____ that he put the note in his pocket unopened.
    A. Tea and biscuits                    B. A cricket match
    C. A chess game                        D. A mystery novel

# Revolutionary War: People—Answer Sheet

1. **B.** **Much greater than.**

2. **B.** **A traitor.** Mobs almost burned down Benjamin Franklin's house during the Stamp Act crisis. When the Stamp Act was first enacted, Franklin was in England and assumed everyone would have to accept the new tax, so he bought tax stamps for his newspaper. When the people of Philadelphia found out what he had done, they were angry. Franklin's wife locked herself in an upstairs room of their house, which she had filled with guns and ammunition. However, the incident passed peacefully.

3. **C.** **Wrote a Declaration of Independence.** Thomas Jefferson was enthusiastic about the document but felt that other delegates at the Continental Congress found it upsetting. Approximately a year later, Jefferson wrote the now-familiar Declaration of Independence, and Congress approved it.

4. **C.** **Revere, Dawes, and Prescott.** Most people know Paul Revere made his famous ride, but they are unaware that William Dawes and Samuel Prescott rode as well. The reason these other two patriots have not received the same attention as Paul Revere is because of the famous poem, *The Midnight Ride of Paul Revere,* written by Longfellow. Why Longfellow chose to only write about Paul Revere and not the other two riders is unclear. It might have something to do with the fact that Revere was a silversmith and was well known. Or, it may be that the name Paul Revere has more rhythm and sounds better in a poem.

5. **A.** **Copperplate engraving.** He was not very good at working with copper, and worked at engraving only when he was having financial difficulties.

6. **B.** **The regulars are coming.**

7. **C.** **Did not attend.**

8. **A.** **King.**

9. **C.** **British soldiers, Boston Massacre.** A British soldier was having things thrown at him and was hit several times with a board. Captain Thomas Preston and other British soldiers came to his aid. The crowd continued to assault the soldiers, and eventually the soldiers fired into the crowd, killing five men. This ended the infamous "Boston Massacre." Captain Thomas Preston, along with eight other soldiers, was charged with murder. Future president, John Adams, along with Joshua Quincy, defended the soldiers, and all but two were acquitted by a local jury. Those two were found guilty of manslaughter, but claimed benefit of clergy. This meant they were allowed to make penance instead of being executed. To ensure that they never could use benefit of clergy again, they were both branded on the thumbs. If they were ever to go to court again, they would need to raise their hands in order to swear an oath to tell the truth. When they did, the brands would be revealed. This was how the custom of raising one's hand in court when one is sworn in came into being.

10. **B.** **Cash. Tobacco was more valuable.** Henry lost the case.

11. **C.** **John Hanson.** George Washington was a general and was fighting in the Revolutionary War when the thirteen American colonies joined together under the Articles of Confederation and decided the new country needed a leader. The Continental Congress elected John Hanson, representative from Maryland, as "President of the United States in Congress Assembled." This was before America had won its independence from England. George Washington had a great deal of respect for

47

Hanson and wrote him a letter of congratulations. Washington even addressed Hanson as President of the United States. After serving for one year, ill health forced Hanson to resign. Two American presidents descended from the Hanson family. They were William Henry Harrison, the ninth President of the United States, and his grandson, Benjamin Harrison, the twenty-third President of the United States.

From 1781 until 1789 when Washington became president, seven men in addition to John Hanson presided over the Congress and were considered President of the United States. However, George Washington became the first President of the United States under the U.S. Constitution in 1789.

12. **B. She carried water in a pitcher to the soldiers.**

13. **D. Unknown.** There are no written records that confirm the legend that Betsy Ross designed the first American flag. The legend began when her grandson told the story in 1870. He said that Betsy had told him the story when he was a child. While records of the time reveal no evidence to support her claim, they do show she was paid to make flags for the Pennsylvania navy in 1777.

14. **C. A chess game.** The note was found when the general was mortally wounded in the subsequent battle.

Name: ____________________ Date: ____________

N I I T S H T O Y

W O N I O T I A T T

U R T A R N E P Y R

A N X E A S T E Z

## A Revolutionary War Slogan

After the French and Indian War, England wanted to recover some of the cost of the war from the colonists. The British felt it was reasonable to have the colonies pay a share for their own defense. The Stamp Act of 1765 was one method the British chose to raise money from the colonies. The colonists were enraged. They rioted and formed the Stamp Act Congress. The Stamp Act was repealed, but other new taxes were levied to take its place. The colonists continued to object strongly to these new taxes. They were not only upset that they were being taxed, they were upset that they had no say in the matter because they had no representatives in the Parliament of England. These concerns turned into a slogan that became popular as the country headed toward the Revolutionary War.

Do you know the slogan? It is hidden in the frame around the page. To discover the slogan, you must go around the frame twice, reading every ***other*** letter. Where do you start, and which way do you read around the frame? That's what you have to figure out. Write the slogan on the lines below.

______________________________________________

______________________________________________

Name: ______________________ Date: ______________

Y M A A W N O F

A L S L A A D E E R

M R A O N B D E I R S

S S I A U W G T

## A Mystery From History

### THE MYSTERY OF ROBERT SHURTLEFF

The young soldier known as Robert Shurtleff was a loner. Maybe he was a loner because his fellow soldiers made jokes about him being so young. His voice had not fully changed and he didn't even shave yet. Robert's comrades also joked about his shyness. Rarely joining in group activities, Robert preferred to spend a lot of time alone. One thing Robert's fellow soldiers didn't joke about, though, was his courage. Fighting bravely, Robert was wounded twice. His first wound was a bullet that remained lodged in his thigh. He was sent to the hospital, but before he could be examined by doctors, he sneaked out of the hospital and dug the bullet out of his own leg. The second time Robert was wounded, the doctor examined him and discovered why he was such a loner. Can you figure it out?

The answer to the mystery is hidden in the frame. To discover the answer, you must go around the frame twice, reading *every other* letter. Where do you start and which way do you read around the frame? That's a mystery too. Write the answer on the line below.

Answer: ______________________________

Name: _____ Date: _____

# The Constitution

The Constitution generally defines the laws of the U.S. federal government. It describes the basic rights of U.S. citizens and explains the three branches of the federal government and outlines their powers. While the Constitution defines how our government operates, it is really only a set of general principles that are used to develop specific laws and procedures. The general nature of the document makes it possible for the legislative or judicial branch of government to interpret the Constitution so that it reflects changing situations and events. At other times, interpretation of the Constitution is set by precedent or custom. In this sense, people have described the Constitution as a "living document."

It is also considered a living document because it can be changed. In fact, it has been changed many times. The Articles of Confederation, ratified in 1781, was the first written Constitution of the United States. In 1787, delegates met in Philadelphia to amend the Articles of Confederation. The Articles were basically rewritten, resulting in the current Constitution. It was submitted to the 13 states for ratification. By June of 1788, nine states had ratified the Constitution. Since 1789, 27 amendments have been added to the Constitution. The first ten amendments were adopted in 1791.

Read each of the unusual facts about the Constitution of the United States in the following sentences and circle the letter before the correct answer.

1. Benjamin Franklin was heavily involved in designing the Constitution's system of representative government for the United States. He used the concepts of justice and liberty he learned from:
   A. The Iroquois Indians.                    B. England.
   C. France.                                  D. The Greeks.

2. Although the 19th Amendment, which became law in 1920, gave every American woman the right to vote, some women could vote in 1776. Who were they?
   A. Wives of plantation owners              B. Women living in New Jersey
   C. Wives of governors                      D. Wealthy women in Philadelphia

3. The Constitution of the United States does not provide citizens the right to:
   A. A speedy trial.                          B. Vote for the president.
   C. Free speech.                             D. A public trial.

4. Who wrote nine of the first ten amendments to the Constitution?
   A. James Madison                            B. Thomas Jefferson
   C. Charlton Heston                          D. Benjamin Franklin

5. Not until 1913, when the seventeenth amendment was passed, could citizens:
   A. Vote if they were 18.                    B. Vote for president.
   C. Vote for representatives.                D. Vote for senators.

Name: _____   Date: _____

6.  In 1923, Upton Sinclair, a well-known novelist, went to jail for reading:
    A. A Harry Potter book.                          B. *The Holy Bible.*
    C. "The Bill of Rights."                          D. "The Battle Hymn of the Republic."

7.  Which word is not found in the Constitution?
    A. Justice                                        B. Slavery
    C. Taxes                                          D. Magazines

8.  The first ten amendments to the Constitution are familiarly known as:
    A. "The Bill of Rights."                          B. "The Top 10 List."
    C. "The Bill of Lading."                          D. Amendments.

9.  Originally, the Constitution said the vice president would be the candidate who:
    A. Received the most votes.                       B. Received the second-most votes.
    C. The winning president chooses.                 D. Was selected by his party.

10. The only crime defined in the U.S. Constitution is:
    A. Perjury.                                       B. Piracy.
    C. Murder.                                        D. Treason.

11. In 1874, Joseph Greeler from Boston presented the U.S. Constitution, the Bill of Rights, and all of the amendments in a special way. What exactly did he do?
    A. Dramatized them                                B. Set them to music
    C. Wrote a ballet about them                      D. Wrote them in the form of a limerick

12. Who advised Benjamin Franklin in 1744 to unite the colonies into a confederacy?
    A. John Jay                                       B. Thomas Jefferson
    C. Jefferson Davis                                D. Chief Cannassatatego

13. What language did Thomas Paine have to learn in 1774 when he traveled to study democracy?
    A. Iroquois                                       B. French
    C. Greek                                          D. Portuguese

14. The second amendment to the Constitution of the United States may well be the one with which most people are familiar. The second amendment gives citizens of the United States the right to:
    A. Bear children.                                 B. Bear arms.
    C. Bare arms.                                     D. Arm bears.

15. Of the following choices, what is the most recent amendment to the Constitution?
    A. Establishing the voting age at 18              B. Repeal of prohibition
    C. Limiting presidents to two terms               D. Right to a speedy trial

# The Constitution—Answer Sheet

1. **A.** **The Iroquois Indians.**

2. **B.** **Women living in New Jersey.** New Jersey had given women the right to vote in 1776. Actually, the new constitution of New Jersey did not specifically say that women had the right to vote. What it said was that any free person worth more than 50 pounds could vote. So if a woman had 50 pounds, she was able to vote. The men who wrote the constitution did not expect women to take advantage of the vote, and at first they were right. Few women voted. However, over the years women began to vote more and more, and they began to decide close elections. In 1807, the New Jersey legislature rescinded the law that made it possible for women to vote.

3. **B.** **Vote for the president.** The president is selected by the Electoral College. At first members of the electoral college were appointed by the state legislatures. In 1832, people began to vote for the electors. Presidential names did not appear on ballots until 1897. Electors generally cast their vote the way the citizens vote, but they are not legally bound to do so. They can vote for whomever they wish, even for the person who receives the least votes. Ordinarily the electors of a state all vote for the candidate receiving the most votes in that state. So if one candidate receives 51 percent of the vote and the other candidate receives 49 percent of the vote, the one receiving 51 percent receives *all* of the electoral votes from that state. This practice caused Rutherford B. Hayes and Benjamin Harrison to be elected in spite of the fact that they had lost the popular vote.

4. **A.** **James Madison.**

5. **D.** **Vote for senators.**

6. **C.** **"The Bill of Rights."** Sinclair was a writer who ran for governor of California. Sinclair read "The Bill of Rights" aloud while speaking to a group of striking transport workers. He had just read the first amendment, which guarantees freedom of religion, speech, press, and the right to peaceably assemble, when the police arrested him. The Los Angeles police charged him with communicating ideas intended to cause hatred and contempt of the U.S. Government. He was released 22 hours later.

7. **B.** **Slavery.**

8. **A.** **"The Bill of Rights."**

9. **B.** **Received the second-most votes.** The Constitution originally said that the person getting the most votes from the state's electors would be president and the one with the second-most would be vice president. This method of selecting the vice president was changed by the 12th Amendment to the Constitution.

10. **D.** **Treason.**

11. **B.** **Set them to music.**

12. **D.** **Chief Cannassatatego.**

13. **A.** **Iroquois.**

14. **B.** **Bear arms.**

15. **A.** **Establishing the voting age at 18.**

Name: _____ Date: _____

# George Washington

Commander in chief of the Continental Army during the American Revolution, George Washington gained the respect of his soldiers, officers, and fellow Americans. He was considered an honest man and an excellent general. While he was loved and respected during his lifetime, after his death his reputation has grown even more. Many of the myths concerning Washington were written in a book by Mason L. Weems. The book was called, *The Life and Memorable Actions of George Washington.* Weems was an Episcopalian minister who had lost his church because of his opposition to slavery. He was a guest speaker at churches, and after he would finish with his sermon, he would go out into the congregation and sell his book about George Washington. It sold so well that he decide to write another and include many more stories and anecdotes about Washington. Some contend that several of the stories that Weems included in his book were made up in order to make the book sell well. Among the stories he included in the second book was the story of how as a child Washington had chopped down the cherry tree. According to the story, Washington then told his father that he could not tell a lie, and confessed that he had chopped the tree down with his hatchet.

See how much you really know about George Washington. Read each of the following sentences and circle the letter before the correct answer.

1.  George Washington had dentures (false teeth) made of:
    A. Wood.                                      B. Steel.
    C. Ivory.                                     D. Ebony.

2.  Washington was the first president to see people:
    A. Fight with muskets.                        B. Elect a president.
    C. Flying.                                    D. Use a steel plow.

3.  The story about George Washington chopping down the cherry tree and then telling his father, "I cannot tell a lie. I chopped down the cherry tree with my hatchet":
    A. Is true.                                   B. Did not happen.
    C. Happened to his brother.                   D. Happened but it was a plum tree.

4.  Washington was born on:
    A. February 11.                               B. February 12.
    C. February 22.                               D. February 30.

5.  President George Washington gave a great deal of his wife's silverware to the government so that it could be:
    A. Sold to finance the war.                   B. Melted and made into combat medals.
    C. Made into dentures for poor children.      D. Melted down and made into coins.

Name:_____ Date:_____

6.  President George Washington was the only president to be elected by:
    A. A direct vote of the people.          B. Secret ballot.
    C. Back door referendum.                 D. A unanimous electoral vote.

7.  Washington was the only president inaugurated on:
    A. Wall Street.                          B. His birthday.
    C. A train.                              D. His promise to reduce taxes.

8.  During her husband's presidency, Martha Washington was formally addressed as:
    A. Madam President.                      B. Lady Washington.
    C. Her excellency.                       D. Marty.

9.  President George Washington created a medal to recognize merit in enlisted men and noncommissioned officers. The medal is known as the:
    A. Medal of Honor.                       B. Distinguished Service Cross.
    C. Purple Heart.                         D. Golden Kazoo.

10. Washington would sometimes do this for three hours at a time:
    A. Powder his wig.                       B. Fence.
    C. Go riding with his grandchildren.     D. Dance with the same woman.

11. Colonel Louis Nicola suggested that Washington become:
    A. A U.S. citizen.                       B. King.
    C. A reading tutor.                      D. A foreign ambassador.

12. Washington was the only president who didn't live in:
    A. Virginia                              B. The state he was registered to vote in
    C. The fear of impeachment               D. Washington, D.C.

13. Washington was the only founding father to:
    A. Become president.                     B. Own a plantation.
    C. Command that his slaves be freed.     D. Never have owned slaves.

14. Which of the following accomplishments should *not* be credited to George Washington?
    A. Introduced the mule to America        B. Brewed beer
    C. Most Supreme Court nominations        D. Longest inaugural address

15. Washington was the first president to:
    A. Marry while president.                B. Resign the presidency.
    C. Have an attempt made on his life.     D. Sponsor an Easter egg hunt.

# George Washington—Answer Sheet

1. **C.** **Ivory.** George Washington did not take care of his teeth and lost them when he was young. He had only one bicuspid at his inauguration. His dentures were not made of wood, as legend has it. They were hippopotamus, deer, horse, and human teeth screwed into an ivory base. Some were made of ivory or lead. He had a special set of dentures made, and in order to keep them from smelling, he soaked them in wine each night. This softened and blackened them.

2. **C.** **Flying.** He watched Jean Pierre Blanchard give a balloon demonstration in Philadelphia.

3. **B.** **Did not happen.**

4. **A.** **February 11.** George Washington was not born on February 22, as is commonly believed. He was born on February 11. In 1752, Great Britain and its colonies dropped the Julian calendar and adopted the Gregorian calendar. Washington's birthday was adjusted to fit into the new system.

5. **D.** **Melted down and made into coins.**

6. **D.** **A unanimous electoral vote.**

7. **A.** **Wall Street.**

8. **B.** **Lady Washington.**

9. **C.** **Purple Heart.**

10. **D.** **Dance with the same woman.**

11. **B.** **King.** Colonel Nicola was a respected officer who complained that Congress did not seem to be accomplishing much. He felt that republics were weak and the only way for the country to survive would be if Washington were to become king. He even suggested a title: King George I of the United States. Washington told Nicola not to mention his idea again either to him or anyone else.

12. **D.** **Washington, D.C.** The White House did not exist when Washington was president. President Washington held a contest for the best architectural design of a "President's Palace." Among those competing was Thomas Jefferson, who among other things, was an architect. Jefferson entered his design under a false name so that no one would know it was he who submitted the design. Jefferson's design didn't win. An Irish architect named James Hoban won the prize of $500 and some land. Of course, the greatest prize for Hoban was the honor of having the future U.S. presidents live in a house he had designed. President Washington never lived in the White House, as it would eventually be named. He died on December 14, 1799, one year before it was completed.

13. **C.** **Command that his slaves be freed.** Washington's will provided for the emancipation of his slaves when his wife Martha died.

14. **D.** **Longest inaugural address.** Actually, his second inaugural address is the shortest on record: 135 words.

15 **C.** **Have an attempt made on his life.** There was a plot to kill George Washington. Thomas Hickey, a member of Washington's guard, devised a plot to poison a plate of peas and serve them to Washington. Hickey asked Phoebe Fraunces to help him. Instead, when she handed the peas to Washington, she told him they were poisoned. He threw them out the window.

Name: _____ Date: _____

# The Louisiana Purchase

The French fur trader and explorer Rene Robert Cavelier, sieur de La Salle, planted a cross at the mouth of the Mississippi River in 1682 and claimed a huge portion of land in the middle of North America in the name of France. The land stretched from the Gulf of Mexico in the south to Canada in the north, and included land on both sides of the Mississippi. He named the land Louisiana, in honor of King Louis XIV.

Over the years, French settlers came to this area to farm and look for gold and silver. While most settled in or near New Orleans, some established villages along the Mississippi. The greatest part of Louisiana, however, was unexplored and uninhabited by Europeans. Even when England defeated the French in the French and Indian War and took Canada and all of the French territory east of the Mississippi River all the way down to the Gulf of Mexico, little was known about this area. Although the English took control of the part of Louisiana east of the Mississippi, France kept the area west of the Mississippi. The English also gained control of Florida, which extended all of the way to the east bank of the Mississippi.

As a result of the French and Indian War, Louisiana was ceded to Spain. In 1800 Spain returned Louisiana to France by the Treaty of San Ildefonso. Napoleon then sold Louisiana to the United States in 1803. This transaction is known as the Louisiana Purchase.

Here are some strange and unusual facts about the Louisiana Purchase. Read each of the following sentences and circle the letter before the correct answer.

1. From 1754 to 1763, France fought England for control of the continent in a conflict called the French and Indian War. England won the war. The English took possession of all the French territory east of the Mississippi River all the way down to the Gulf of Mexico. They did not take the part of Louisiana that was west of the Mississippi because they:

   A. Wanted to avoid conflicts with Spain.     B. Viewed it as worthless.

   C. Didn't have manpower to defend it.     D. Didn't know it belonged to France.

2. The French King, Louis the XV, gave the remaining part of Louisiana to his cousin, Charles III of Spain because Spain had:

   A. Given France the recipe for hot crepes.     B. Just celebrated its sesquicentennial.

   C. Owned territory to the west.     D. Fought on the side of the French.

3. In Louisiana in the middle part of the eighteenth century, British traders were:

   A. Forbidden to enter Louisiana.     B. The only source for tea and crumpets.

   C. Sold franchises for "Fish and Chips."     D. The only traders permitted.

4. In 1784, the Spanish closed the lower Mississippi to:

   A. Indians.     B. All foreigners.

   C. Americans.     D. Mimes.

Name: _____ Date: _____

5.  In 1793, the French decided to make a scientific expedition west of the Mississippi River. Thomas Jefferson indicated he felt that in this vast wilderness there might be:
    A. Dinosaurs.                                    B. Johnny Appleseed.
    C. Butterflies the size of eagles.                D. Llamas and huge mammoths.

6.  In 1797, President John Adams sent three envoys to France to diplomatically resolve the differences between the two countries. French officials tried to get the envoys to pay a bribe in exchange for ceasing hostilities. Adams was angry and called the whole situation the:
    A. X, Y, Z Affair.                                B. Tallyrand's Folly.
    C. Money for Peace Initiative.                    D. Adam's Apple.

7.  In the early part of the 1800s, the King of Spain, King Charles IV, was so ignorant and had such little interest in political matters that he didn't know:
    A. The name of the King of France.               B. Who owned Louisiana.
    C. Columbus was Italian.                          D. The American Revolution had occurred.

8.  King Charles IV, the King of Spain, spent his days hunting and playing. His hunts lasted over six hours. On his hunts, he took over:
    A. 10 aides.                                      B. 100 aides.
    C. 1000 aides.                                    D. 10,000 aides.

9.  When King Charles IV, the King of Spain, wanted to relax, he enjoyed:
    A. Repairing watches.                             B. Jacks.
    C. Blind Man's Bluff.                             D. Creating mazes.

10. One of the things that bothered President Jefferson about the Louisiana Purchase was the fact that it:
    A. Was so expensive.                              B. Was unconstitutional.
    C. Was an unknown territory.                      D. Contained those huge mammoths.

11. Jefferson was considered the greatest real estate broker in America because he bought Louisiana:
    A. For about three cents an acre.                 B. Without paying a sales commission.
    C. With no money down.                            D. Before Spain knew it was for sale.

12. Jefferson was not really interested in purchasing Louisiana; he was mainly interested in purchasing:
    A. Bourbon Street.                                B. Quebec.
    C. New Orleans.                                    D. French Guiana.

Name: _____ Date: _____

# The Louisiana Purchase—Answer Sheet

1. **B.**   **Viewed it as worthless.** In fact, most Europeans viewed this land as just a wilderness without any value.

2. **D.**   **Fought on the side of the French.** This was a gift because Spain had helped fight England during the French and Indian War. Spain's King at first did not want to accept this large part of North America. Like England, they thought it had little value. Spain was irritated because it had lost Florida to England because of its part in the French and Indian War. However, Spain accepted the gift rather than anger France. Also, Spain was afraid that England would grab the land for itself. One thing Spain did like in the deal, though, was that it included New Orleans, the port that controlled the Mississippi River traffic.

3. **A.**   **Forbidden to enter Louisiana.** It was rarely enforced, however. In fact, there were British boats that were called floating stores on the Mississippi River, selling everything from food to hardware.

4. **B.**   **All foreigners.** Of course foreigners meant Americans, as well as everybody else.

5. **D.**   **Llamas and huge mammoths.**

6. **A.**   **X, Y, Z Affair.** The three envoys were Charles Pinckney from South Carolina, Elbridge Gerry from Massachusetts, and John Marshall from Virginia. They were kept waiting for two weeks before Tallyrand, who was the Directory's Minister of Foreign Affairs, would see them. When French government officials tried to get America to pay a bribe in order to stop the hostilities, they refused. They returned to the United States and made a report to the President. Instead of using the names of the officials who asked for bribes, the letters X, Y, and Z were substituted.

7. **D.**   **The American Revolution had occurred.** King Charles spent his days hunting and playing.

8. **C.**   **1,000 aides.**

9. **A.**   **Repairing watches.** King Charles IV also liked working as a carpenter, playing card games, playing the violin, praying, napping, and forging armor.

10. **B.**   **Was unconstitutional.** The U.S. Constitution made no provision for acquiring new land and giving citizenship to inhabitants living outside the United States. Jefferson admitted that the purchase was an act beyond the Constitution and he had no legal authority to approve the purchase. He worried that if Congress did not ratify the sale, Napoleon might change his mind and back out of the agreement. Jefferson even considered a constitutional amendment to make it legal. The amendment was not needed. The treaty was ratified on October 20, 1803.

11. **A.**   **About three cents an acre.**

12. **C.**   **New Orleans.** Jefferson was concerned that the French controlled the Mississippi River. He sent James Monroe and Robert R. Livingston to Paris to negotiate the purchase of a tract of land on the lower Mississippi, including New Orleans. If that was unsuccessful, Monroe was to negotiate the right to navigate on the river free of charge. The negotiators were surprised by the French offer to sell the whole territory. They immediately negotiated the treaty.

Name: _____    Date: _____

# A Mystery From History
## THE TECUMSEH CURSE

In September of 1811, two Indian leaders, Tecumseh and his half-brother, Prophet, attempted to unite the Shawnee Indian tribes. At the time, American leaders thought this might be a British attempt to stir up Indians on the U.S. borders. Remember, this was just before the War of 1812. So in order to stop this potential Indian problem, Congress sent Governor William Henry Harrison, who would eventually become President of the United States, to deal with it.

Harrison and his army marched against Prophet's town, and in the battle of Tippecanoe killed many Shawnees and sacked the town. In a later battle, he killed Prophet. Tecumseh joined the British, and in the war of 1812 fought against the Americans.

Harrison was elected as President of the United States in 1840, and legend has it that Tecumseh hated Harrison and the United States so much because of how the Indians were treated that he had placed a curse on Harrison. The curse supposedly applied not only to Harrison but to every president elected in a year that ends in "0," just as Harrison was. Specifically, the curse says that every president who is elected in a year that ends in "0" will die in office.

It is a nice, interesting legend. There is just one problem with this legend; there is no historical evidence that Tecumseh ever placed a curse on Harrison or on any future president. The legend probably began because of a play in 1836. There was a scene in the play that had Tecumseh dying on a battlefield. In one of his final speeches during the play, Tecumseh cursed Harrison. Of course, the play was fiction, and there was no evidence that Tecumseh ever actually cursed Harrison. Probably everyone would have forgotten all about it if something strange hadn't happened in 1840 and again in 1860 and again and again. Sure, it's fiction, but it is still interesting and a little eerie just the same. Fill in the blanks below, and you'll see what I mean.

1. In 1840, _____ was elected President of the United States. He died of _____ after serving _____ days in office.

2. _____ years later, in 1860, _____ was elected President of the United States. During his second term in 1865, he was _____.

3. _____ years later, in 1880, _____ was elected President of the United States. He was _____. He died several months later.

4. _____ years later, in 1900, _____ was reelected President of the United States. In 1901 he was _____. He died 8 days later.

5. _____ years later, in 1920, _____ was elected President of the United States. In 1923, he was sitting in the White House when he _____.

6. _____ years later, in 1940, _____ was reelected President of the United States. During his third term in 1945, he died of _____.

7. _____ years later, in 1960, _____ was elected President of the United States. In 1963, he was _____.

8. _____ years later, in 1980, _____ was elected President of the United States. In 1981, he was _____, but he did *not* die. Does this end the curse? Or was it all just a coincidence?

Name: _____ Date: _____

# The Cherokee Nation

The Cherokee Nation is the name given to a tribe of North American Indians that lived in the mountainous region of the western Carolinas, northern Georgia, and eastern Tennessee before the Europeans came to America. They were the largest and most powerful group of Indians in the region. They had a very well-developed and highly-organized society. The white settlers described them as honest, smart and industrious.

Every Cherokee town had seven clans which were separated by lines of sticks or stones. The clans were actually extended families. The clan consisted of parents, brothers and sisters, grandparents, aunts and uncles, and cousins. The clan took responsibility for the well-being of all of its members.

Several Cherokee tribes helped the British during the American Revolution and continued to resist the settlers until the late 1700s. After this time, they began to adopt the settlers' culture and customs. They developed farms. They grew vegetables, cotton, and corn and raised pigs, cattle, and horses.

In 1838, the U.S. government forced the Cherokee to leave their homeland and march to what is now Oklahoma. Of the approximately 15,000 involved in the march, it is estimated that 4,000 died. This march is called the "Trail of Tears."

See how much you know about the Cherokee Nation. Read each of the following sentences and circle the letter before the correct answer.

1.  The Cherokee Nation established a form of government very similar to:
    A. The Sioux.                            B. The Greeks.
    C. The Romans.                           D. The U.S. government.

2.  The Cherokee man Sequoya, also known as George Gist, did something no human had ever done before. What was it?
    A. Created a written language            B. Ran the mile in four minutes
    C. Climbed Pike's Peak                   D. Ate three dozen jalapeño peppers

3.  Which of the following did the Cherokee *not* have in 1838?
    A. Constitution                          B. Newspaper
    C. Gambling casino                       D. Official records

4.  The Cherokees wrote the first Indian newspaper in 1828. It was called the *Cherokee Phoenix*. It was unusual because it was:
    A. Written on bark.                      B. Written in sign language.
    C. Written in English and Cherokee.      D. The first to carry Little Orphan Annie.

5.  In the early part of the nineteenth century, some Cherokees:
    A. Owned villas in Mexico.               B. Owned African slaves.
    C. Began relocating to India.            D. Participated in the Olympic Games.

Name:_____     Date:_____

6.  In the early part of the nineteenth century, most Cherokees wore:
    A. Loin cloths.                          B. Kilts.
    C. European clothes.                     D. Clothes made from deerskin.

7.  In the early part of the nineteenth century, many Cherokees were:
    A. Christians.                           B. Jews.
    C. Atheists.                             D. Cherokists.

8.  In the early part of the nineteenth century, most Cherokees wore:
    A. Feathers in their hair.               B. Ten-gallon hats.
    C. Toupees.                              D. Turbans.

9.  When a Cherokee man and woman married, they lived with:
    A. The husband's family or clan.         B. A clan that was different from either.
    C. The wife's family or clan.            D. No one else.

10. Cherokees whitewashed their homes with lime, which they made by crushing burnt:
    A. Animal teeth.                         B. Animal bones.
    C. Discarded piano keys.                 D. Clam shells.

11. Each Cherokee town had:
    A. One chief.                            B. Two chiefs.
    C. Three chiefs.                         D. Four chiefs.

12. When the Removal Act was passed in 1830, the Cherokee nation:
    A. Fought it in court.                   B. Went on the warpath.
    C. Did nothing.                          D. Accepted it.

13. In the Cherokee family, who was considered the head of the household?
    A. Man                                   B. Woman
    C. Child                                 D. Chief

14. In the Cherokee family, who owned most of the property?
    A. Man                                   B. Woman
    C. Children                              D. Chief

15. Cherokee children belonged to the:
    A. Father.                               B. Mother.
    C. Grandparents.                         D. Chief.

Name:_____ Date:_____

16. Traditionally, Cherokee children were taught by the:
    A. Father.                          B. Mother.
    C. Schoolmaster.                    D. Mother's brothers.

17. When a child was sick, he or she would be taken to a shaman. The shaman was the head of the council and advised people on spiritual and medical concerns. If the shaman was unable to cure the child, the shaman would take the child to a stream or lake and:
    A. Wash away evil spirits.          B. Drown him.
    C. Give him a new name.             D. Baptize him.

18. For the first two years of a Cherokee child's life, how often was he bathed?
    A. Weekly                           B. Daily
    C. Monthly                          D. Never

19. When a Cherokee died, he was buried beneath:
    A. The tribal lodge.                B. A totem pole.
    C. A sacred elm tree.               D. The place of death.

20. Each year the Cherokees held a ceremony where they:
    A. Destroyed their possessions.     B. Danced for rain.
    C. Celebrated Columbus Day.         D. Prayed for a bountiful harvest.

21. Which of the following were *not* needed to play a game of lacrosse?
    A. An elderly man to oversee        B. Someone to whoop
    C. A person to sing                 D. A play-by-play announcer

22. The night before a lacrosse game, the players:
    A. Prayed to the Great Spirit.      B. Went over scouting reports.
    C. Planned their strategy.          D. Bathed seven times.

23. The day of a lacrosse game, the players were scratched with:
    A. Pine cones and needles.          B. Porcupine quills.
    C. Rattlesnake fangs or turkey quills. D. Pumice.

24. Which of the following weapons did the Cherokees *not* use?
    A. Blow guns                        B. Bow and arrows
    C. Boomerangs                       D. Spears

25. John Ross, Chief of the Cherokees, had a house:
    A. With a two-car garage.           B. With hot running water.
    C. Designed by a Philadelphia architect. D. With walk-in closets.

# The Cherokee Nation—Answer Sheet

1. **D.** **The U. S. government.** The Cherokees imitated the white man in many ways.
2. **A.** **Created a written language.** Sequoya observed that white men had the ability to communicate through time and space by making marks on special leaves, so he designed a written language based on syllables that fit with the existing spoken Cherokee language.
3. **C.** **Gambling casino.**
4. **C.** **Written in English and Cherokee.** Just before their removal it is estimated that 90 percent of Cherokee males could read and write their own language; many of them could also read and write English.
5. **B.** **Owned African slaves.** Since many Cherokees had adopted the European ways, it is not surprising that they also adopted the practice of owning slaves.
6. **C.** **European clothes.**
7. **A.** **Christians.**
8. **D.** **Turbans.**
9. **C.** **The wife's family or clan.** Since men were away hunting much of the time, women played a vital role in Cherokee society. They even participated in the government.
10. **D.** **Clam shells.**
11. **B.** **Two chiefs.** There was the White Chief, also known as the most-beloved man, who handled the daily business of the town. The other was the Red Chief, who dealt with fighting, war parties, the victory dances, and games.
12. **A.** **Fought it in court.**
13. **B.** **Woman.**
14. **B.** **Woman.**
15. **B.** **Mother.**
16. **D.** **Mother's brothers.**
17. **C.** **Give him a new name.** It was decided that the patient's name was no longer any good, so a new name was needed.
18. **B.** **Daily.**
19. **D.** **The place of death.** He was buried either beneath the place of death, under the hearth, or just outside the house. The Cherokee's belongings were buried with him or burned at his grave site.
20. **A.** **Destroyed their possessions.** They liked to prove how little possessions meant to them.
21. **D.** **A play-by-play announcer.** A group would send a challenge to another town. Once the challenge was accepted, the town needed an elderly man to oversee the game, a singer for the players, someone to whoop, and a musician for seven women who danced on the seventh night of preparations for the game.
22. **D.** **Bathed seven times.**
23. **C.** **Rattlesnake fangs or turkey quills.** This was done to toughen them up for the game.
24. **C.** **Boomerangs.**
25. **C.** **Designed by a Philadelphia architect.**

Name: _____ Date: _____

# Texas and War With Mexico

The war between the United States and Mexico is often touched on only briefly in some textbooks. However, this was an important conflict because of what resulted when the fighting ended and a peace treaty was signed; Mexico not only recognized the U.S. annexation of Texas, but it ceded California and an area of land in the Southwest that now includes several states.

Shown below are some strange and little-known facts about the Texas war for independence and the war with Mexico. Read each of the following sentences and circle the letter before the correct answer.

1. After his victory at the Alamo, General Santa Anna, commander of the Mexican forces, was later overthrown from his dictatorship and exiled from Mexico to:
   A. Hoboken, New Jersey.              B. Arizona.
   C. Staten Island, New York.          D. Chile.

2. Some of the best fighters in the Mexican army were:
   A. Deserters from the American army.  B. German mercenaries.
   C. Argentinian peasants.              D. Cuban refugees.

3. A Mississippi rifleman remarked that the Mexican troops were:
   A. Rotten soldiers with rotten leaders.  B. Too pretty to shoot.
   C. The best that money could buy.        D. Like a pack of spoiled brats.

4. Antonio Lopez de Santa Anna, the Mexican leader of the Alamo attack, was instrumental in inventing:
   A. Chewing gum.                       B. Mexican jumping beans.
   C. The repeating rifle.               D. The Macarena.

5. William Tecumseh Sherman suggested that the United States go back to war with Mexico in order to force Mexico to:
   A. Take New Mexico and Arizona back.  B. Make its citizens leave Texas.
   C. Relinquish all of Mexico.          D. Stop bullfighting.

6. The Americans called Santa Anna:
   A. Blood and Thunder.                 B. Old Wooden Leg.
   C. Santa Anita.                       D. Mexicali Rose.

7. Winfield Scott was a general in the American army. He was called:
   A. Old Rough and Ready.               B. Old Fuss and Feathers.
   C. Winnie Scott.                      D. Pumtooty.

Name: _____ Date: _____

8. Mexican generals were concerned that their soldiers might desert their posts, so they would sometimes:

    A. Have guards watch the soldiers.        B. Make them take an oath not to desert.

    C. Provide coffee and cake at the front.    D. Chain the soldiers to their cannons.

9. Between 1833 and 1855 there were _____ changes in the Mexican presidency, _____ of which were held by Santa Anna.

    A. 36, 11                           B. 5, 3

    C. 15, 5                           D. 52, 28

10. When Sam Houston's wife left him, he resigned as governor of Tennessee and went to live:

    A. In California.                    B. In a cave.

    C. With Cherokee Indians.         D. In Houston, Texas.

11. General Ulysses S. Grant called the Mexican War the most:

    A. Glorious of America's wars.       B. Exciting time of his life.

    C. Complete training for a soldier.    D. Unjust war "America had ever fought."

12. When Abraham Lincoln was a congressman, he protested the war with Mexico by:

    A. Withholding his poll tax.         B. Refusing to eat tacos.

    C. Resigning from the army.        D. Picketing the White House.

13. Sam Houston was Texas's senator for two and a half terms. He was forced out when he refused to:

    A. Line dance.                      B. Support secession from the Union.

    C. Send soldiers to defend the Alamo.    D. To negotiate with Santa Anna.

14. The popular song *The Yellow Rose of Texas* refers to:

    A. A Texas belle named Savannah.    B. A slave girl named Emily.

    C. A flower growing on Houston's grave.  D. San Antonio.

15. The treaty annexing Texas to the Union says that Texas had a right to:

    A. Divide into as many as five states.    B. Become a state of Mexico at any time.

    C. Change its borders at will.         D. Make Spanish the legal language.

16. Texas was actually ruled under:

    A. Four flags.                      B. Six flags.

    C. Eight flags.                 D. Ten flags.

# Texas and War With Mexico—Answer Sheet

1. **C.** **Staten Island, New York.**
2. **A.** **Deserters from the American army.**
3. **B.** **Too pretty to shoot.** Santa Anna's troops were elaborately dressed in uniforms of various bright colors. They wore silken banners and plumes. By contrast, the American troops were led by General Zachary Taylor, who was dressed like a farmer. He wore a broad-brimmed straw hat, a duster, and odd-looking pantaloons.
4. **A.** **Chewing gum.** Santa Anna was in exile in Staten Island, New York, in 1869. He had a piece of sap from the sapodilla tree, which Mayan Indians often chewed. He gave a piece of the sap to Thomas Adams, who was his interpreter and secretary. Adams tried many different experiments, and then he finally decided to separate the sap into small balls and add sweetening and flavors. He later began the Adams Chewing Gum Company.
5. **A.** **Take New Mexico and Arizona back.** William Tecumseh Sherman hated the American Southwest so much that he suggested that the United States go back to war with Mexico in order to force Mexico to take New Mexico and Arizona back.
6. **B.** **Old Wooden Leg.** Santa Anna lost a leg defending Veracruz. He became a national hero. The cork leg was found in a carriage by Illinois troops at Cerro Gordo. Santa Anna had escaped by horse.
7. **B.** **Old Fuss and Feathers.** He was given this nickname because of his emphasis on appearance and discipline.
8. **D.** **Chain the soldiers to their cannons.**
9. **A.** **36, 11.** Between 1833 and 1855, Mexico had 36 changes in presidency, 11 of which were held by Santa Anna.
10. **C.** **With Cherokee Indians.** Houston was 35 when he married an 18-year-old woman, Eliza Allen. She left him after three months. Neither Eliza nor Sam would reveal why she left. There were many rumors that he may have mistreated her, or that he became depressed and resigned as governor. He went to Arkansas and stayed with the Cherokee Indians he had spent three years with when he was a teenager. He drank heavily but eventually left the tribe and moved to Texas. When he was 47, he married 21-year-old Margaret Lea. They remained married until Houston died at age 70. Eliza, Houston's first wife, also remarried.
11. **D.** **Unjust war "America had ever fought."**
12. **A.** **Withholding his poll tax.** A poll tax is an amount levied against each adult in a particular location. The poll tax was not only used as way for the government to acquire money, but also to keep certain groups from voting. At one time, the U.S. poll tax made it impossible for poor black people to vote. If they couldn't pay the tax, they couldn't vote. The poll tax for federal elections was eliminated by the twenty-fourth amendment to the United States Constitution. In 1966 the Supreme Court outlawed the poll tax in state elections.
13. **B.** **Support secession from the Union.**

# Texas and War With Mexico Answer Sheet

14. **B.** **A slave girl named Emily.** General Santa Anna took a slave named Emily from the household of Colonel James Morgan and made her his companion. On April 21, 1836, at San Jacinto, Texas, Santa Anna and Emily were drinking champagne when Sam Houston's Texans attacked the Mexican force. Santa Anna was so involved with Emily that he was not prepared for the attack. While there were only 800 Texans, they either killed or captured 1,500 Mexicans. Emily became famous for her part in the defeat of Santa Anna. The song lyrics have changed many times over the years.

15. **A.** **Divide into as many as five states.**

16. **B.** **Six Flags.** It is generally accepted that six national flags have flown over Texas since the first Europeans arrived on this continent.

## The Six Flags of Texas

**Texas Under Spain**
**1519–1685; 1690–1821**

**Texas as a Republic**
**1836–1845**

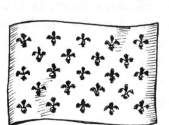

**Texas Under France**
**1685–1690**

**Texas in the Confederacy**
**1861–1865**

**Texas Under Mexico**
**1821–1836**

**Texas in the United States**
**1845–1861; 1865–Present**

Name: _____  Date: _____

# Gold Rush

The greatest gold rush in the history of the United States began with the discovery of gold at Sutter's Mill on the American River in northern California in 1848. While some prospectors came immediately when the gold "strike" was announced, it wasn't until 1849 that the real "rush" began. People came not only from all around the United States, but from all over the world. Not only prospectors, but farmers, merchants, and artisans also swarmed to the area. Gold production provided money for an expanding California, as well as the American economy. There was capital as well as a demand for goods. Railroads and wagon roads were needed. California's population grew from about 14,000 in 1848 to 380,000 by 1860.

The California gold rush of 1849 and the Comstock Lode silver strike in 1859 were responsible for San Francisco's growth. Close to the mines, San Francisco was the destination not only of Americans who arrived by sea or overland, but it was also the destination of waves of immigrants who arrived to work the mines and in related jobs. Manufacturing and service industries flourished. Chinese, Japanese, Italian, and Filipino communities were established.

See if you are able to answer some of the strange and bizarre facts about the gold rush of 1849. Read each of the following sentences and circle the letter before the correct answer.

1. Who was the person who discovered gold in the American River near John Sutter's sawmill in California in 1848?
   A. John Sutter
   C. Michael Midas
   B. Ruby Tuesday
   D. James Wilson Marshall

2. When gold was found on his land, John Sutter asked his workmen not to tell anyone about the discovery for six weeks so that he could:
   A. Have time to file a claim.
   C. Purchase goods to sell prospectors.
   B. Check to see if the gold was real.
   D. Do his spring planting.

3. During the gold rush of 1849, people who went to California in search of gold were called:
   A. Argonauts.
   C. Gold diggers.
   B. Gold seekers.
   D. 49ers.

4. At first, Marshall and Sutter weren't sure if the original nugget that was found was gold, so they:
   A. Dipped it in acid.
   C. Took it to an assayer.
   B. Checked it out in an encyclopedia.
   D. Took it to the bank.

5. When news of the gold discovery in Sutter's Creek reached San Francisco, it was ignored because there was a bigger story about:
   A. President Lincoln's assassination.
   C. The discovery of copper deposits.
   B. President Johnson's impeachment.
   D. Lincoln's image found on Rushmore.

Name: _____ Date: _____

6. In order to reach the gold fields as quickly as possible, the editor of the newspaper, *Scientific American*, suggested that someone build:
   A. A canal from St. Louis to California.
   B. A flume from St. Louis to San Francisco.
   C. An elevated train.
   D. An aerial locomotive.

7. The first *large* group of people who came to the California gold rush were from:
   A. Hawaii.
   B. Mexico.
   C. New England.
   D. Canada.

8. During the gold rush, Australia sent many _____ to San Francisco.
   A. Kangaroos
   B. Convicts
   C. Dingoes
   D. Burros

9. The gold rush gave John Sutter, the man on whose land the gold was originally found:
   A. Pain and anguish.
   B. The richest mine in California.
   C. A prosperous mining store.
   D. A successful bed and breakfast inn.

10. John Marshall, the man who originally found gold in Sutter's Creek, became part of the gold rush. When he died he was:
    A. Rich and famous.
    B. Poor and alone.
    C. At his villa in Italy.
    D. Governor of California.

11. In the mining camps, saloon owners would hire bartenders who:
    A. Were good fighters.
    B. Were able to lift a barrel of whiskey.
    C. Had big fingers and thumbs.
    D. Could sing in a barbershop quartet.

12. Some prospectors brought along:
    A. Metal detectors.
    B. Gold-sniffing dogs.
    C. Diving suits.
    D. Gophers to dig for gold.

13. There were so many people traveling to California on the trails, that there were:
    A. Traffic jams.
    B. Traffic cops.
    C. Many bed and breakfast inns.
    D. Many quick-food inns.

14. When a man was caught stealing something of little value in a mining camp, he was usually flogged. Sometimes afterwards the onlookers would:
    A. Flog the one who reported the crime.
    B. Shout "one more time."
    C. Execute the thief.
    D. Take up a collection for the thief.

15. Where could a miner stake a claim?
    A. Anywhere he wanted
    B. Only on private land
    C. Only on public land
    D. Anyplace except Indian land

Name: _____ Date: _____

16. One of the things miners did for entertainment was to:
    A. Watch a baseball game.        B. Watch a fight between a bear and a bull.
    C. Play bingo on Saturday night.      D. Hold dance-a-thons.

17. When gold was originally discovered in Sutter's Mill in 1848, there were nearly 1,000 people living in San Francisco. After news of the gold strike became well known, how many remained in San Francisco?
    A. 100        B. 1,000
    C. 10,000      D. 100,000

18. It was common for crews to desert their ships as soon as they hit San Francisco Bay in order to go and try to find gold. At one time there were _____ ships in San Francisco Bay that had been abandoned, sunk, or beached because crews could not be found.
    A. 20        B. 120
    C. 520      D. 1,020

19. The streets of San Francisco, which were not paved, became so muddy that people began throwing things in them to make them more stable. Abandoned ships were unloaded and their contents dropped into the streets. On one occasion, a whole shipload of _____ was thrown into the streets and eventually sank through the mud.
    A. Logs        B. Cooking stoves
    C. Sand      D. Pianos

20. Miners enjoyed watching:
    A. Plays by Shakespeare.        B. Silent movies.
    C. Other miners becoming successful.      D. Mimes.

21. Criminals from Australia who lived in San Francisco were called:
    A. Aussie Bugs.        B. Britain's Rejects.
    C. Sydney Ducks.      D. Jailbirds.

22. San Francisco was growing so rapidly, and wood and labor were so scarce, that some people used _____ for buildings.
    A. Tepees        B. Caves
    C. Conestoga wagons      D. Deserted ships

# Gold Rush—Answer Sheet

1. **D.** **James Wilson Marshall.** Sutter owned the land, but he had hired James Wilson Marshall to build and operate a sawmill on his land. During construction, Marshall found a gold nugget and took it to Sutter.

2. **D.** **Do his spring planting.** He wanted to have a chance to get his spring planting done before all of his workers started to leave in order to look for gold.

3. **A.** **Argonauts.** The term "49ers" was not used at the time the rush was on. It became popular later.

4. **B.** **Checked it out in an encyclopedia.**

5. **C.** **The discovery of copper deposits.**

6. **D.** **An aerial locomotive.** The editor of the newspaper *Scientific American*, Rufus Porter, suggested that someone build an aerial locomotive. It was to be a large balloon propelled by steam engines. Rufus Porter thought that such a machine would be able to travel at a speed of 100 miles per hour. It was never built.

7. **A.** **Hawaii.** The first large group of people who came to the California gold rush were from Hawaii. News of the gold discovery arrived on the Hawaiian Islands from sailors. It took less time to come from Hawaii than it did to cross the American continent.

8. **B.** **Convicts.** Australia, which had been a prison colony for Great Britain for many years, sent many convicts to San Francisco just to get rid of them. This increased the crime problem in San Francisco.

9. **A.** **Pain and anguish.** The gold rush did little for John Sutter, the man on whose land the gold was originally found. Prospectors descended upon his land, stole his livestock, let their horses and oxen graze in his fields of grain, and trampled his other crops. Sutter eventually moved away with almost nothing to show for the years he had spent building a fortune on his land. When he tried to get reimbursement from the U.S. government, there were many legal problems because some of his land grants had come from the Mexican government. Eventually, he received a pension of $3,000 a year from the state of California. He moved to Pennsylvania.

10. **B.** **Poor and alone.**

11. **C.** **With big fingers and thumbs.** They wanted someone with big fingers and thumbs because the price of a drink was a pinch of gold dust.

12. **C.** **Diving suits.** Some prospectors brought along diving suits in order to walk along the bottom of the deep streams and pick up nuggets.

13. **A.** **Traffic jams.** There were so many people traveling to California on the trails, that there were, indeed, traffic jams. There were carts pulled by oxen and mules that were backed up for miles as the prospectors trudged toward California.

14. **D.** **Take up a collection for the thief.** Miners realized that the guilty needed to be punished in order to discourage others from committing the same crime. But they also knew that stealing food or something of little value was usually done by someone who was very hungry and very poor. So they sometimes took pity on the criminal, and after the man had been flogged, the onlookers would take up a collection to provide the thief with enough money to move to another camp.

# Gold Rush—Answer Sheet

15.  **A.**  **Anywhere he wanted.** A miner could stake a claim anywhere. It didn't matter if it was on someone's farm, in his yard, or in the town. He could stake his claim with four pegs, and the land was his as long as he worked on it. Usually he was required to work at least one day per month.

16.  **B.**  **Watch a fight between a bear and a bull.** This was a cruel sport that was imported from Mexico. A chained grizzly bear was put into an arena and a bull was turned loose; the two would then fight.

17.  **A.**  **100.**

18.  **C.**  **520.**

19.  **B.**  **Cooking stoves.**

20.  **A.**  **Plays by Shakespeare.** Edwin Booth, the brother of John Wilkes Booth, the man who assassinated Abraham Lincoln, was a Shakespearean actor who performed at many mining camps.

21.  **C.**  **Sydney Ducks.**

22.  **D.**  **Deserted ships.** There were hundreds of abandoned ships in San Francisco Bay because the crews had left to look for gold. It seemed logical to beach them and use them as buildings. They were used as stores, warehouses, a church, a bank, and one was even a prison.

73

Name: _____ Date: _____

# The Civil War
## BATTLES

The U.S. Civil War was a war of many firsts. There were many new, technically advanced weapons introduced, including armored warships. Much of the horror of many of the battles was photographed by Mathew B. Brady.

See how much you know about some of the battles of the Civil War. Read each of the following sentences and circle the letter before the correct answer.

1. One of the most famous naval battles of the Civil War was between:
   A. The *Monitor* and the *Virginia.*
   B. The *Monitor* and the *Merrimack.*
   C. The *Constitution* and the *Independence.*
   D. The *Lusitania* and the *Titanic.*

2. The Union ironclad, *Monitor,* was the first U.S. ship to have a:
   A. Mounted cannon.
   B. Commander who was an admiral.
   C. Plate of armor.
   D. Flush toilet.

3. Union general, John Sedgwick was killed at the battle of Spotsylvania in 1864. He was watching the Confederate troops. His last words were:
   A. It looks like he's aiming at me ...
   B. They couldn't hit an elephant at this dis ...
   C. Come on boys. It's clear.
   D. Hey, Reb. You still out there ...

4. The 2nd Virginia Regiment frantically searched a battlefield for something they wanted very badly. They were looking for:
   A. Guns and ammunition.
   B. Shoes.
   C. Band instruments.
   D. Soft tack.

5. The *C.S.S. Hunley* was a submarine used in the Civil War. Its claim to fame was that it was the first submarine to:
   A. Fight in a war.
   B. Sink an enemy ship.
   C. Use a kerosene engine.
   D. Carry a crew of 20.

6. The Battle of Shiloh took place at:
   A. Shiloh.
   B. Gettysburg.
   C. Jerusalem Falls.
   D. Pittsburgh Landing.

7. During the Civil War, this was needed for each battle.
   A. A Gattling gun
   B. A cannon
   C. A band
   D. A cheerleading squad

Name: _____    Date: _____

8.  Which of the following was not used in the Civil War?
    A. Flame thrower                        B. Aircraft carrier
    C. Land mines                           D. Gas-operated machine gun

9.  On June 18th, 1861, the gas-filled balloon called the *Enterprise* demonstrated that balloons could be used as a military weapon to provide information about enemy troops. The people in the balloon demonstrated that they could not only see the enemy troops 15 miles away, but could send this information to the people below by:
    A. Dropping written messages.          B. Homing pigeon.
    C. Telegraph.                           D. Sign language.

10. In some cases, a Civil War battle might have two different names, the reason being that Confederates named battles after nearby towns while Union troops often named battles after:
    A. Nearby mountains.                    B. Nearby streams.
    C. Nearby churches.                     D. Generals.

11. Mark Twain served in the Confederate Army for two weeks before he:
    A. Deserted.                            B. Was wounded.
    C. Transferred to Mexico.               D. Was killed.

12. Secretary of War Jefferson Davis ordered 70 of these animals to be brought to the United States in 1856. They were to provide transportation for military personnel until the transcontinental railroad was built.
    A. Llamas                               B. Elephants
    C. Burros                               D. Camels

13. The first Union shot of the Civil War at Fort Sumter was fired by:
    A. U.S. Grant.                          B. Pvt. John Wayne.
    C. James Naismith.                      D. General Abner Doubleday.

14. Confederate General Richard Ewell thought he was:
    A. A descendant of Columbus.            B. A bird.
    C. Not appreciated by Lee.              D. Underestimated by Union forces.

15. General Ulysses S. Grant would not move his army unless he was supplied plenty of:
    A. Whiskey.                             B. Ammunition.
    C. Onions.                              D. Horses.

# The Civil War: Battles—Answer Sheet

1. **A.   The *Monitor* and the *Virginia*.** The *Monitor* never fought the *Merrimack*. The *U.S.S. Merrimack* was a Union ship that was set on fire and sunk when northern forces abandoned the Norfolk Navy Yard in 1861. The Confederates raised the *Merrimack,* covered it with armor plating, and rechristened the ship the *C.S.S. Virginia.* So the well-known sea battle we read about in history books was actually fought between the *Monitor* and the *Virginia.*

2. **D.   Flush toilet.**

3. **B.   They couldn't hit an elephant at this dis ...**

4. **C.   Band instruments.** The 2nd Virginia Regiment was able to form a band from instruments taken from a New York unit after a battle.

5. **B.   To sink an enemy ship.** Although the *C.S.S. Hunley*, a Confederate ship, was not America's first submarine, it was the first to sink a warship. The *Hunley* was made from a cylindrical iron steam boiler that held a crew of nine sailors. One steered the boat, and the other eight powered the vessel by cranking the propeller by hand.

    On February 16, 1864, the *Hunley* attacked the *U.S.S. Housatonic*, in Charleston Harbor off the coast of South Carolina. The *Hunley* had a metal canister on a rod extending from the submarine. The canister had 100 pounds of gunpowder designed to enter the enemy ship's wooden hull. The *Hunley* rammed the *Housatonic* with the torpedo, backed away about 130 feet, and detonated the bomb. The attack was successful, and the *Housatonic* was sunk. Unfortunately, the *Hunley* was not able to get far enough away, and the explosion that sunk the *Housatonic* also sank the *Hunley.*

6. **D.   Pittsburgh Landing.** The Battle of Shiloh actually took place at Pittsburgh Landing, Tennessee. It was called Shiloh because it was near Shiloh Church, which was named after a place north of Jerusalem.

7. **C.   A band.** Throughout the Civil War, a band was needed for each battle. Music encouraged the soldiers to fight. During the Battle of Gettysburg, the music got so loud that a North Carolina regiment's band was shot at by Union soldiers. By 1862 there were 618 bands in the Union at a cost of $4 million. There was an average of one musician for every 41 soldiers. The Confederacy had fewer bands because they didn't have as much money. At night, there would often be concerts at the front; both sides would listen and applaud.

8. **D.   Gas-operated machine gun.** On August 1st, 1861, a balloon used to estimate Confederate troop strength was launched from a transport ship called "Fanny." This is the first recorded example of using a sea vessel to launch an airship. Consequently, it was an aircraft carrier.

    The Confederate Army had fewer balloons in service. The first Confederate balloon accession was made by Lt. John Randolph Bryan. The flight did not last long, because the enemy began firing at the balloon. Bryan immediately brought the balloon back to earth. His first response was to resign from ballooning; however, General Johnson refused to let him resign

9. **C.   Telegraph.** A thin wire wrapped in green silk spun off of a reel on the ground as the balloon floated up to 500 feet. Then the telegraph key on the ground began to click. A message from the balloon was being sent.

# The Civil War: Battles—Answer Sheet

10. **B.** **Nearby streams.** Here are examples of battles with different names:

| Union Name | Confederate Name |
|---|---|
| Antietam | Sharpsburg |
| Bull Run | Manassas |
| Fair Oaks | Seven Pines |
| Stones River | Murfreesboro |
| Elkhorn Tavern | Pea Ridge |

11. **A.** **Deserted.**

12. **D.** **Camels.** The western wagon route from Texas to California was dry, hot, and similar to the Middle East where camels had been used for transportation for centuries. Jefferson Davis proposed a Camel Military Corps, and Congress appropriated $30,000 to the venture. When the camels reached America, they were tested. They were loaded with 600 to 800 pounds each and traveled 25 to 30 miles a day. They worked well with little food or water. The project seemed to work for about two years, then when the Civil War began, the Camel Military Corps was dissolved. The camels were auctioned off, but a few escaped into the desert.

13. **D.** **General Abner Doubleday.** Doubleday is often incorrectly given credit for inventing baseball. According to the legend, Doubleday invented the game of baseball when he was a schoolboy in Cooperstown, New York.

14. **B.** **A bird.** He would only eat a few grains of wheat or sunflower seeds at a meal. He also spent a great deal of his time in his tent chirping. He was a brave soldier who lost a leg at the Second Battle of Bull Run in 1862. Eventually, his health failed.

15. **C.** **Onions.** General Ulysses S. Grant had been a farmer and believed that onions would prevent dysentery and other physical ailments. He is said to have sent the following message to the War Department: "I will not move my army without onions." Within a day, the U.S. government sent three trainloads of onions to the front.

Name: _____     Date: _____

# Civil War Cube Puzzle

Find the answer to the puzzle hidden in the letters below. The answer begins with the circled letter (U) and ends with circled letter (N). Follow a vertical, horizontal, or diagonal path from the first letter to the last and the answer will be spelled out. Do not cross your path. Each letter is used only once. You can use the blanks shown below to record your answer. The first and last letters are already filled in for you.

| A | B | I | Ⓝ |
|---|---|---|---|
| C | Ⓤ | N | A |
| Y | S | C | L |
| M | O | T | E |

Puzzle : Abraham Lincoln once said this was one of the causes of the Civil War.

U__ __ __ __    __ __ __ __    __ __ __ __ N

78

Name: _____ Date: _____

# A Mystery From History
## ENLISTING IN THE ARMY

Variations of this story were common during the Civil War. While it can't be documented, it is likely that it did happen in some communities.

Edwin Lansdown lived on small farm in west central Illinois. His big ambition was to join the Union Army and fight to preserve the Union. Early one morning he dressed, grabbed his rifle and set out for Quincy, Illinois, in order to enlist. He arrived at the recruiting tent in Johnson Park just a little after lunch. There was a short line of young men waiting to enlist. The recruiting sergeant was a tough-looking man with a full black beard.

"Say, boy," Edwin heard the sergeant roar at the boy in the front of the line. "Jist how old are you?"

Edwin recognized the boy. It was Jeremy Rushing. They both attended the same church.

Jeremy straightened up, looked the sergeant straight in the eye, and said, "I'm over eighteen, Sir."

Edwin couldn't believe his ears. He knew that Jeremy was the same age as he was—sixteen. He also knew that Jeremy would never lie. Not for any reason.

The sergeant looked at Jeremy skeptically and then said. "Okay, boy. Go over to that other tent and they'll sign you up."

As Jeremy passed Edwin, Edwin grabbed him by the arm.

"Jeremy," he whispered. "Why did you lie?"

"Huh?"

"About your age. You ain't eighteen. You're sixteen."

Jeremy looked around to make sure no one could hear him.

"You have to be eighteen to join up." Jeremy whispered. "Anyway, I didn't lie."

"You did too. You're sixteen like me."

"Listen, Edwin. Did you come here to join up?"

"Yes, but I ain't gonna lie. I know better than that. You do, too."

"You don't have to lie. Look, come over here."

Jeremy took Edwin by the arm and led him behind a huge oak tree so that the recruiting sergeant couldn't see them. He sat on the ground, took off his boot, pulled out a piece of folded paper and handed it to Edwin.

"Here, Edwin. Put this in your boot."

Edwin unfolded the paper, read it, and smiled. He sat down next to Jeremy, refolded the paper, and put it his boot as Jeremy had said. He then went and stood in line.

When his turn came, the sergeant asked him the same question he had asked Jeremy.

"How old are you, boy?"

Edwin said, "I'm over eighteen, Sir."

"Are you lyin', boy? This army don't want no liars."

"I'm tellin' the truth, Sir." And he was.

How can this be?

Name: _____ Date: _____

# The Wild West

During the latter part of the nineteenth century, the United States grew with the opening of the West. Unfortunately, the population grew much faster than the pioneers' ability to develop law and order. There was virtually no law west of St. Louis. Certainly there were some marshals and a number of Indian Tribal Police, but not nearly enough to keep order in the territories. Towns and cities would hire a sheriff, if they could afford it. A single sheriff was usually no match for a gang of desperate, vicious criminals, unless, of course, the sheriff was just as mean and vicious. In that case, honest people lived in fear of the criminals as well as the sheriff. The "Wild West" as it has come to be known, was not a very relaxing place to live.

Out of this colorful era arose many myths. See if you are able to separate the truth from the fiction about the "Wild West." Read each of the following sentences and circle the letter before the correct answer.

1.  In the latter part of the nineteenth century, William Thompson, a repairman for the Union Pacific Railroad, presented Dr. Richard Moore with a very unusual gift, which the doctor eventually donated to the Omaha Public Library Museum. It was:
    A. The Transcontinental R.R. gold spike.      B. His scalp.
    C. Bat Masterson's bat.                        D. The world's first baseball card.

2.  In 1860 there were many:
    A. Turkey drives.                              B. Prairie dog barbecues.
    C. Buffalo roundups.                           D. Poetry contests for cowboys.

3.  Bat Masterson, sheriff of Ford County from 1877 to 1881, eventually became:
    A. A train robber.                             B. A congressman.
    C. A sportswriter.                             D. A minister.

4.  The gunfight that took place on October 26, 1881, known as "The Gunfight at the OK Corral" in Tombstone, Arizona territory, lasted about:
    A. Thirty seconds.                             B. Three minutes.
    C. Thirty minutes.                             D. Three hours.

5.  Jesse Wayne Brazel killed Sheriff Pat Garrett of Lincoln County, New Mexico, by shooting him once through the back and once through the head. When he was arrested, he pleaded:
    A. Insanity.                                   B. Mistaken identity.
    C. Accidental death.                           D. Self-defense.

6.  When Tom and Frank McLaury and Billy Clanton were killed in the Gunfight at OK Corral in Tombstone, Arizona, their bodies were:
    A. Displayed in a hardware store window.       B. Stuffed and put in a museum.
    C. Dug up and held for ransom.                 D. Cremated.

Name: _____    Date: _____

7.  From 1906 until 1921, the Rangers in New Mexico were called:
    A. The New Mexico Mounted Police.      B. The New Mexico Rangers.
    C. The Lone Rangers.                   D. The Forest Rangers.

8.  In the West before 1895, the first shot in a gunfight was very important because:
    A. Gunfighters were so accurate.       B. So much smoke was produced.
    C. The noise was so distracting.       D. Ammunition was so expensive.

9.  Sam Bass, a Texas stagecoach robber, always made sure that each passenger he robbed had:
    A. Fare to get home.                   B. At least $1 for breakfast.
    C. Directions to the next station.     D. A parasol to shield them from the sun.

10. When Kit Carson was 14 years old, he was "bound" to a tradesman to learn the craft of:
    A. Corset-making.                      B. Blacksmithing.
    C. Saddle-making.                      D. Hat design.

11. Western movies have shown us that there were saloons, hotels, livery stables, and gambling halls in the Wild West. However, some towns also had:
    A. Bowling alleys and roller-skating rinks.   B. Swimming pools and water parks.
    C. Theme parks.                        D. Buffalo Burger Huts.

12. Once when Jesse James and his gang held up a train, one of the robbers announced that he would only take money from passengers who had:
    A. Fat wallets.                        B. Soft hands.
    C. Worked for the railroad.            D. Money.

13. Once, when Jesse James and his gang held up a train, before he left he handed the conductor:
    A. A press release describing the robbery.   B. Money for his fare.
    C. His gun and pointed a note at him.  D. A picture of himself and his gang.

14. A very small gun was named Reid's "My Friend" Knuckle Buster. It was a .32 caliber gun and was so heavy that it was also used to hit people in the head. The most remarkable feature of this gun, however, is that it did not have a:
    A. Handle.                             B. Trigger.
    C. Bullets that would fit.             D. Barrel.

15. According to Wyatt Earp, the man who would win in a gunfight was the man who:
    A. Had the quickest "draw."            B. Was not afraid to die.
    C. Was the best shot.                  D. Took his time.

# The Wild West—Answer Sheet

1. **B.    His scalp.** In 1867 William Thompson, a repairman for the Union Pacific Railroad, was attacked by Cheyenne Indians. They scalped him, but an Indian accidentally dropped the scalp as he rode away. Thompson grabbed his scalp and went to the doctor's office. The doctor was unable to reattach the scalp, but the wound did heal and Thompson survived. Thompson had the scalp preserved and gave it to the doctor who had treated him. Eventually the scalp was donated to the Omaha Public Library Museum for display

2. **A.    Turkey drives.** Turkeys can run fast, and their meat was valued in the West. On one occasion a man named Henry Hooker, who lived in California, bought a flock of turkeys for $1.50 each. With two dogs to help him, he drove the turkeys to silver miners and sold them for $5 each.

3. **C.    A sportswriter.** Bartholomew (Bat) Masterson was sheriff of Ford County from 1877 to 1881. Legend says that he killed one man for every year that he was alive. While there is no evidence to support this claim, it can be proved that he did kill at least 12 people. In 1902 he moved to New York City and became a sportswriter for the New York City *Morning Telegraph.*

4. **A.    Thirty seconds.** While entire movies have been made about this famous event, it actually only lasted about 30 seconds. The gunfight took place at the OK Corral in Tombstone, Arizona, on October 26, 1881. City Marshal Virgil Earp, along with his brothers Wyatt and Morgan and friend Doc Holliday, exchanged fire with the Clanton and McLaury brothers. Billy Clanton and Tom and Frank McLaury were killed. In the feud that followed, Morgan was later murdered, and Wyatt Earp retaliated by killing three men.

5. **D.    Self-defense.** Pat Garrett was the New Mexico sheriff who found and shot Billy the Kid. When Brazel killed Sheriff Garrett by shooting him once through the back and once through the head, he pleaded self-defense. He said he was so afraid of the former sheriff that he had to shoot him in the back in order to live.

6. **A.    Displayed in a hardware store window.** In the Old West when a lawman caught and killed an outlaw, it was big news. People were very curious and wanted to learn details. One way to satisfy this curiosity was to display the bodies of those killed or to see a photograph of the deceased. A lawman usually photographed the corpse of a criminal he had killed. This was done for identification as well as a souvenir for the lawman. Another important reason to make the photograph and to display it widely was to discourage others from committing crimes.

7. **A.    The New Mexico Mounted Police.**

8. **B.    So much smoke was produced.** The first shot in a gunfight was very important because so much smoke was produced by the first shot that the shooters were often unable to see each other for a second shot.

9. **B.    At least $1 for breakfast.**

10. **C.    Saddle-making.** He later ran away and became a famous scout.

11. **A.    Bowling alleys and roller-skating rinks.**

12. **B.    Soft hands.** He said, "Hard-handed people have to work for their money. The soft-handed ones are capitalists, professors, and others that get money easy."

# The Wild West—Answer Sheet

13. **A.** **A press release describing the robbery.** A *press release* is an announcement someone gives to a newspaper so they will have basic information concerning a story the paper is writing. For example, suppose your class was going to have an ice-cream social. You might send your newspaper an announcement giving details about the event. You would include what the event was called, when it was going to be held, where it was going to be, and other information you felt was important.

While Jesse did not call his note a press release, his note did give details of the robbery he had just committed and read like news articles of the day. Jesse left the amount he had stolen blank since the note was written the night before and he had no idea how much he would get. In addition, he gave false information concerning the robbers' descriptions. Here's what the note said:

*THE MOST DARING ROBBERY ON RECORD*
*The southbound train on the Iron Mountain Railroad was boarded here this evening by five heavily armed men and robbed of _____ dollars. The robbers arrived at the station a few minutes before the arrival of the train, arrested the station agent and put him under guard, then threw the train on the switch. The robbers were all large men, none of them under 6 feet tall. They were all masked and started in a southerly direction after they had robbed the express. They were all mounted on fine, blooded horses. There is a hell of an excitement in this part of the country.*

14. **D.** **Barrel.** It fired directly from the revolver chambers.
15. **D.** **Took his time.** The person who fired first was often very nervous, and his aim was off.

Name: _____     Date: _____

# A Mystery From History
## THE MYSTERY OF JESSE JAMES

We don't know if this is a true story, but there are some who live in the Ozarks who swear that it really did happen. It is stories like this that have led some to view Jesse James as more than just a common outlaw.

Once the famous outlaw Jesse James, his brother Frank, and the Younger brothers were riding in the Ozark Mountains. The outlaws were hungry, thirsty, and tired when they came to a cabin that belonged to an elderly widow who lived alone. The widow peered uneasily through her window as the dusty group of men rode up to her cabin and one came up on the porch. Jesse knocked at the cabin door.

"Sorry to bother you, ma'am," Jesse said. "But our horses are tired and thirsty and we're hungry. Could you fix us something to eat? We'd be happy to pay you."

Although the sight of the men made her nervous and she had little food, she let the men in and began to prepare them a meal. "But I won't take none of your money," she said. "That wouldn't be the Christian thing to do. A person has a duty to help those in need."

As she went about the business of cooking, she spoke little, but the men could see that something was bothering her. They asked her what was wrong. She was reluctant to tell them her problems, but with a little coaxing she revealed that her husband had not been dead for very long, and he had not only left her without money, but had also left her deeply in debt.

"That ain't the worst of it," she said. "The mortgage on my cabin and land is past due and the banker is coming this afternoon for $800. Since I ain't got it, he'll take the farm. And I don't have no place to go."

The men ate in silence. Then when the meal was finished, they huddled together and began talking softly to each other while the woman cleaned the table. After a few minutes, Jesse asked her about the banker. He wanted to know what the banker looked like, how he was traveling, and where he was coming from. The widow was puzzled with his interest, but she answered the questions as best she could.

Finally Jesse said, "You know, ma'am, you have been very kind to us, and we would like to help you out. We want to loan you the money to pay off your mortgage."

The woman was stunned. She began to cry and said she couldn't accept his generosity because she wasn't sure if she would ever be able to pay them back.

"There's no need to worry about that right now," Jesse said. "Whenever you get the money you can pay me." Jesse reached into his pocket, pulled out a wad of bills, counted out $800, and handed it to her. Then Jesse had his brother Frank write her a receipt for the $800 and told the woman to copy the receipt in ink. After she made a copy of the receipt, Jesse said, "Now, when the banker comes, hand him the $800 and make sure that he signs this receipt. This is very important. You must have proof that you paid him. That's the way business is handled. Another thing," Jesse added, "don't tell him we've been here."

The widow agreed to do everything Jesse had told her. Then Jesse and his gang went out to their horses, mounted up, and rode away.

That afternoon, the banker arrived at the cabin. He was surprised that the woman had the $800 to pay her mortgage. He really wanted the farm, but there was nothing he could do. He accepted the money and reluctantly signed her receipt. Then he rode away.

Why would Jesse loan a stranger $800? Can you solve this mystery?

84

Name: _____  Date: _____

# Wagon Trains

During the middle of the nineteenth century, America was growing and expanding westward. This great expansion, which is sometimes referred to as the "great migration" began in 1843. It took place, for the most part, on the Oregon Trail. Over 25 years, more than a half million people loaded up their wagons and traveled west on this exciting but dangerous trail. Some were settlers, some were looking for gold, some went to escape persecution, and some went to seek a new life and new opportunities. The days of the wagon trains largely ended in 1869, when the transcontinental railroad was completed.

Shown below are some strange and little-known facts about traveling west on wagon trains. Read each of the following sentences and circle the letter before the correct answer.

1.  The thing that pioneers traveling west in wagon trains hated most about the *Oto*, *Kansa*, *Kickapoo*, and *Potowatomie* tribes they encountered was:
    A. They would attack at night.          B. They would beg for food.
    C. They would poison their water supply.  D. They had toll bridges.

2.  Sometimes wagon trains wanted to leave a message for future trains. They might give advice such as where water can be found or if the water was bad. They sent their messages by "bone express." Bone express referred to:
    A. Simon Bone who traveled the trail.     B. Letters carved on bones and mailed.
    C. Messages left on sticks or bones.       D. A letter service owned by Daniel Bone.

3.  Those traveling west on wagon trains usually drank a great deal of coffee because:
    A. The caffeine made them alert.          B. The water they encountered was bad.
    C. It was cheap.                           D. Only sissies drank tea.

4.  At least one company of Mormons who moved west transported their supplies and goods not on a regular wagon, but by:
    A. Pulling a two-wheeled handcart.         B. Flatboat.
    C. Helium-filled balloon.                  D. Wind-driven sail wagons.

5.  Wagon trains traveling over the Oregon Trail would move at about:
    A. 1–2 miles per hour.                     B. 3–5 miles per hour.
    C. 6–8 miles per hour.                     D. 9–10 miles per hour.

6.  Of those who traveled west between 1840 and 1860, how many died along the way?
    A. One in two                              B. One in ten
    C. One in a hundred                        D. One in a thousand

Name: _____ Date: _____

7. Most groups of Indians a wagon train encountered wanted to:
   A. Fight to protect their land.          B. Borrow eye shadow.
   C. Remind the settlers not to pollute.   D. Trade.

8. Pioneers would put a bucket of milk on the side of their wagon in order to:
   A. Save room in the wagon.               B. Attract the flies away from them.
   C. Make butter.                          D. Make yogurt.

9. The desert sands and the rough ground sometimes caused the oxen to go lame. In order to avoid this, settlers would often:
   A. Put metal shoes on the oxen.          B. Make booties for the oxen.
   C. Avoid rough ground and deserts.       D. Have the oxen ride in the wagons.

10. People who had made the trip west, experienced the difficult frontier life, decided that they did not like it, and wanted to return home were called:
   A. Go-backers.                           B. Returners.
   C. Losers.                               D. Boomerangs.

11. People who had made the trip west and decided they didn't like it would use the expression:
   A. There's no place like home.           B. I'm shufflin' off to Buffalo.
   C. I have seen the elephant.             D. Goodbye, Seattle. Hello, St. Louis.

12. Usually the meal at midday consisted of leftovers from breakfast. In this way, there was no need to take time to cook. The midday meal was called:
   A. Nooning.                              B. Tea time.
   C. Brunch.                               D. TGIN.

13. One thing children did as they made their journey across the country was to play with:
   A. Hula hoops.                           B. Frisbees.
   C. Pogo sticks.                          D. Homemade scooters.

14. Pioneers who traveled by wagon train to the west coast were referred to as:
   A. Sooners.                              B. Overlanders.
   C. Johnny-come-latelys.                  D. Seattle land hawks.

15. The famous Donner party was lost because it relied upon:
   A. A travel agent.                       B. A real estate promoter.
   C. The *Old Farmer's Almanac.*           D. A map maker.

# Wagon Trains—Answer Sheet

1. **D.** **They had toll bridges.** The prairie had deep ravines created by creeks. The Indians built bridges over these ravines and charged the pioneers to use them. Pioneers used these bridges because they saved time and effort and lessened the possibility of damage to their wagons. But in most cases, the pioneers had used all of their money to purchase their wagons and supplies. This was an expense they hadn't planned on.

2. **C.** **Messages left on sticks or bones.** Settlers taking a wagon train to the West could communicate with relatives back east by sending letters along the way. Sometimes, however, wagon trains wanted to leave a message for future trains. They left these messages posted on sticks or sun-bleached bones. This type of communication was known as the roadside telegraph or the bone express. Sometimes false messages were left as a joke.

3. **B.** **The water they encountered was bad.** Much of the water they found along the trail was polluted, muddy, or foul tasting. The strong flavor of coffee disguised the taste of the water.

4. **A.** **Pulling a two-wheeled handcart.**

5. **A.** **1–2 miles per hour.** Most of the settlers traveled on foot, not on the wagons. The only exception might be a child or someone who was sick.

6. **B.** **One in ten.** Death was very common on these journeys. There were, of course, diseases such as cholera, typhoid, measles, dysentery, and others. Many of these diseases were caused by camping in the same place that others had camped before. With no proper sewage facilities or toilets, the water supplies were often infected with disease. These kinds of diseases were also common in big cities, with a large percentage of people falling ill and dying. Along the trail there were additional dangers. People fell out of wagons and under the wheels, some were drowned while driving a wagon across a river, and accidental shootings were common.

7. **D.** **Trade.** Movies often show that those traveling west were afraid of Indian attacks. They show great battles and a lot of bloodshed; however, this was not common. For the most part, Indians either ignored those traveling west or they traded with them.

8. **C.** **Make butter.** The bouncing of the wagon would turn the milk into butter by the end of the day.

9. **B.** **Make booties for the oxen from rawhide.**

10. **A.** **Go-backers.**

11. **C.** **I have seen the elephant.**

12. **A.** **Nooning.**

13. **B.** **Frisbees.** They weren't the plastic frisbees we are familiar with today; they used buffalo dung. The Great Plains region was covered with buffalo chips. While children sailed them from time to time, they were mainly burned for fuel.

14. **B.** **Overlanders.**

15. **B.** **A real estate promoter.** The famous Donner party was lost because an emigrant guidebook was in error. The 1846 wagon train was snowed in by an early winter storm and trapped in the mountains until their rescue in February of 1847. They had relied upon a traveler's guide published by a California real estate promoter.

Name: _____    Date: _____

# A Mystery From History
## AVOIDING CHOLERA

When Seth Scott saw Joe Campbell in the saloon in Seattle, he was happy. Joe had been the wagon master on the train when Seth and his family had come west over the Oregon Trail. In fact, it was Joe who had encouraged Seth to become a wagon master and help other families come to the west coast, just as Joe had helped Seth and his family.

"How's it goin', Joe? How was your trip?"

"Fine, when you get in?"

"Last week. Lose many?"

It was not a rude question. Those who brought wagon trains across the country were very concerned with the safety of the pioneers they led. It was a dangerous journey and many died. On average, one in ten died on each wagon train that came across the country. There were some accidents, but disease claimed most of the victims on the trail. It was a matter of pride among those who led the trains along the trail to lose as few as possible. It was something to brag about.

"Two," Joe said, "Out of one hundred and fifty-eight." He gave a slight smile of pride.

"Only two?" Seth asked. He was skeptical.

"Yep. One drowned, the other got shot by accident. A few got the measles, but they didn't die."

"Come on, Joe. How about cholera and other sickness?"

Seth knew that cholera, typhoid, dysentery, and other diseases usually took a heavy toll on those traveling west on wagon trains. The pioneers weren't sure of the causes of these diseases, but today we know many of these illnesses are caused by bacteria that thrive in unsanitary conditions. The pioneers traveled the same trails and camped where others had camped before. With no proper sewage facilities or toilets, the water supplies were often infected with these bacteria.

"Nope," Joe continued, "Last trip I didn't have nobody die of cholera. I found out how to stop it—a secret formula."

If Seth hadn't known Joe, he would have thought Joe was joking or lying. Deaths from cholera and other diseases were common on wagon trains; it was an accepted risk of the trip. But he knew that Joe never joked or lied.

"Secret formula?"

"Yep," Joe continued. "It's coffee. That's the secret."

"Coffee?"

"Yep. I don't let nobody drink nothin' but coffee on the trip. Strong coffee. The stronger the better. Since I started makin' everybody only drink coffee, I had only a few get sick. Must be somethin' in the coffee that stops it."

Seth was skeptical, but he decided to try Joe's plan. On his next trip, Seth would not allow anyone to drink anything but coffee—even the children. To Seth's surpise, it worked. Not one person died from cholera on his trip to Seattle.

Why do you think this worked? Was there something in the coffee that stopped cholera, or was it just a coincidence?

Name: _____ Date: _____

# Pioneer Life

After the War of Independence, pioneers began to move west and settle in the frontiers of North America. In the 1700s the frontier of North America was the Appalachian Mountains. At a later time, pioneers traveled west across the Mississippi River and eventually to California and Oregon.

The pioneers moved to the frontier for many different reasons. They all wanted an opportunity to start new lives. Many of the pioneers were homesteaders. Others came to the frontier because they had heard stories that made it sound as if it were easy to become rich in this vast, unexplored territory. There were prospectors, hunters, and trappers. There were also craftsmen, doctors, lawyers, and businessmen.

Shown below are some strange and little-known facts about pioneer life. Read each of the following sentences and circle the letter before the correct answer.

1. During the first half of the nineteenth century, it was estimated there were between 15 and 20 million buffalo on the western plains of North America. By the middle of the 1890s, there were less than:
   A. 10.                                          B. 100.
   C. 1,000.                                       D. 10,000.

2. In California's Sierra Nevada, between 1861 and 1865, mail was delivered by:
   A. Pony Express.                                B. Balloon.
   C. Llamas.                                      D. Dog sled.

3. In 1868, this person was the first woman to vote in a presidential election.
   A. Lucy Garfield                                B. Charlotte Parkhurst
   C. Carry Nation                                 D. Mildred Fillmore

4. In 1845, Congress passed a law that enabled postmasters to create postage stamps. Revenue from the stamps would pay for the postage to deliver the letter to the post office. The person receiving the letter would:
   A. Show identification to get it.               B. Wait until the first of the month to get it.
   C. Wait until it was delivered on Monday.       D. Pay an additional fee to get it.

5. Who brought wheat farming to Kansas?
   A. Mennonites from Russia                       B. Amish from Germany
   C. Phillis Wheatley                             D. Spanish

6. Bismarck, North Dakota, was named to after:
   A. Indian Chief Bismark.                        B. Governor Billy Joe Bismark.
   C. Wild Bill Bismark.                           D. Germany's Otto von Bismarck.

Name: _____  Date: _____

7. Between 1854 and 1929, there were orphan trains that ran between New York and the West. They were called orphan trains because:
   A. They were filled with orphans.
   B. There was only one train per week.
   C. They had no conductors.
   D. The company was named "Orphan."

8. Between 1870 and 1883, many buffaloes were killed and their bones left on the plains. People known as "bone pickers" would gather these bones and sell them to companies who used them to make fertilizer and:
   A. Museum exhibits.
   B. Dice.
   C. Bone china.
   D. Piano keys.

9. The pioneers traveling across the country did their laundry with a homemade soap called lye soap. The soap was made from a liquid called lye that was made from:
   A. Pumice.
   B. Borax.
   C. Cold cream and perfumes.
   D. Ashes.

10. Most houses in the West used windows made of:
    A. Glass.
    B. Quartz.
    C. Greased paper.
    D. Buffalo hides.

11. This was used as wallpaper in the Old West.
    A. Old newspapers.
    B. Pages from the Sears Catalog.
    C. Velour.
    D. Circus posters.

12. The term "prairie coal" referred to:
    A. Sagebrush.
    B. Dead trees.
    C. Onyx.
    D. Buffalo or cow chips.

13. Indian police officers were often called:
    A. Range ranger.
    B. Metal breasts.
    C. Indian patroller.
    D. White man's dog.

14. "Batwings" were a type of:
    A. Chaps worn by cowboys.
    B. Indian war bonnet.
    C. A fashionable shawl worn by women.
    D. A favorite dish eaten by pioneers.

15. When Zebulon Pike was in south central Colorado, he saw something that looked like "the sea in a storm, except as to the color." To what was he referring?
    A. The ocean
    B. The Great Salt Lake
    C. The Great Sand Dunes of Colorado
    D. Zoysia grass

# Pioneer Life—Answer Sheet

1. **C.** **1,000.** Many were killed for their hides and others for sport. After the animal was skinned, the rest of the buffalo was left to rot on the plains.

2. **D.** **Dog sled.**

3. **B.** **Charlotte Parkhurst.** Actually, Charlotte went by the name of Charlie Parkhurst. She was a stagecoach driver whom everyone thought was a man. She dressed and acted as a man, was very tough, and had a reputation for bringing her stages in on time. Once she was held up and killed two of the bandits. People thought she was strange since she was always clean-shaven and preferred to stay away from other people and to sleep alone. When Charlie died in 1879, everyone found out the truth. It was revealed that she originally wore men's clothing to escape from an orphanage.

4. **D.** **Pay an additional fee to get it.** The revenue from the postage stamp only paid for delivery of the letters to the post office.

5. **A.** **Mennonites from Russia.** When the Mennonites came to Kansas in 1874, they brought with them a hearty winter wheat seed that they had used in the Ukraine in Russia. They planted the wheat, and in the first year there was a drought and a plague of locusts. The corn crop was lost, but the wheat survived. This was the beginning of wheat farming in Kansas.

6. **D.** **Germany's Otto von Bismarck.**

7. **A.** **They were filled with orphans.** In 1854 there were many poor and abandoned children living on the streets of New York City. These children either came from institutions, or were children whose parents could not afford to keep them. At the same time, there were families living out west who wanted children. The Children's Aid Society would round up orphans on the streets in New York, give them baths and fresh clothes, and send them west for adoption. Once they arrived, people would line up and select the child they wanted. Although some people only adopted children to work as unpaid laborers, many of the adoptions worked out very well for the children. Living on the streets of New York was very dangerous, and there was little hope that they could survive for very long. Many successful people were originally some of these orphans who had been sent west. In fact, two governors, Andrew Burke of North Dakota and John Brady of the Alaskan Territory, were orphans who were sent west.

8. **C.** **Bone china.**

9. **D.** **Ashes.**

10. **C.** **Greased paper.** It allowed light to enter the house. Glass windows were very expensive.

11. **A.** **Old newspapers.** It was inexpensive and provided reading material for the family.

12. **D.** **Buffalo or cow chips.**

13. **B.** **Metal breasts.**

14. **A.** **Chaps worn by cowboys.**

15. **C.** **The Great Sand Dunes of Colorado.**

Name: _____ Date: _____

# Schools in Early America Logic Problem

Schools were organized early in the colonies. In 1647, the Massachusetts colony ordered every village with more than 50 families to have a public school. As pioneers traveled west, education was not given the priority it was in New England. Food, shelter, clothing, and protection from Indians and wild animals were uppermost on the minds of the pioneers. Children had to work in order for the family to have the necessities of life and to survive. Only after these basics of life were met was education considered. Eventually, settlements on the frontier began to establish a system of education.

On the frontier, men taught winter sessions while women often taught the shorter summer sessions. Schoolmasters might be very smart or they might be ignorant. Farmers would sometimes teach in order to make money in the winter when they couldn't farm. Since there was little money in pioneer villages, teachers were not paid very well. Often they were paid with hams, pumpkins, hides or other commodities. They were sometimes "boarded" from one house to another. This means the teacher would live with each family who had a child for a period of time, often a week. The family would give him a place to stay and feed him. In exchange, the teacher was expected to help with the chores. After the week was over, the teacher would move and "board" with another family.

Solving this logic problem dealing with schools in early America is fun but challenging. All the information you need to solve the problem is given either in the introduction or in the clues. In addition to using the clues, you must also use logic to solve the problem. In order to solve the problem, you may use the solution chart on the next page. Write "yes" in the appropriate box on the chart when you discover a correct answer and "no" when you are sure that the box represents an incorrect answer. Sometimes, as you work through the problem and fill out the solution chart, you may get stumped and need to guess at an answer. If you do guess, you can test the guess to see if it would work out with the clues you were given. If you discover your guess is incorrect, you can always change it on the solution chart.

## CLUES

1. Irving wanted to become a lawyer and thought that the skill that Mr. Skinner taught him during the fourth week of his circuit would help him when he spoke to a jury.

2. The student in Pittsfield was studying a subject so that he would be able to keep his father's books in his business. He did not study his lessons during the second or fifth weeks.

3. During the first week, Mr. Skinner visited Hull and taught reading to a girl with a long name.

4  Christian was the student taught when Mr. Skinner visited Griggsville, just after his stay in Hull.

5. The reason the student in Kinderhook chose the course of study she did was because she was an admirer of Phillis Wheatley. Mr. Skinner taught in Kinderhook the week after he taught Irving.

Name: _____ Date: _____

# Schools in Early America Solution Chart

| | Griggsville | Kinderhook | Pittsfield | Pleasant Hill | Hull | Edith | Irving | Christian | Savannah | Henrick | Reading | Writing | Arithmetic | Geography | Declamation |
|---|---|---|---|---|---|---|---|---|---|---|---|---|---|---|---|
| First Week | | | | | | | | | | | | | | | |
| Second Week | | | | | | | | | | | | | | | |
| Third Week | | | | | | | | | | | | | | | |
| Fourth Week | | | | | | | | | | | | | | | |
| Fifth Week | | | | | | | | | | | | | | | |
| Reading | | | | | | | | | | | | | | | |
| Writing | | | | | | | | | | | | | | | |
| Arithmetic | | | | | | | | | | | | | | | |
| Geography | | | | | | | | | | | | | | | |
| Declamation | | | | | | | | | | | | | | | |
| Christian | | | | | | | | | | | | | | | |
| Irving | | | | | | | | | | | | | | | |
| Edith | | | | | | | | | | | | | | | |
| Savannah | | | | | | | | | | | | | | | |
| Henrick | | | | | | | | | | | | | | | |

| Week | Village | Student | Subjects Studied |
|---|---|---|---|
| First | | | |
| Second | | | |
| Third | | | |
| Fourth | | | |
| Fifth | | | |

Name: _____  Date: _____

# World War II

World War II began in Europe on September 1, 1939, when Germany attacked Poland. The United States was brought into the war on December 7, 1941, when the Japanese attacked the U.S. naval base at Pearl Harbor, Hawaii. The United States declared war on Japan the following day, and on December 11 Germany and Italy declared war on the United States.

One side in the conflict was called the "Allies." It included the United States, Great Britain, France, China, and the U.S.S.R. The other side—the side that lost the war—was called the "Axis." It included Germany, Japan, and Italy. The war formally ended on September 2, 1945, with the formal surrender of Japan aboard the U.S. battleship *Missouri* in Tokyo Bay.

See if you know some of the strange and bizarre facts about World War II. Read each of the following sentences and circle the letter before the correct answer.

1. The original last name of Adolf Hitler, the ruler of Germany from 1933 to 1945, was:
   A. Himmler.
   C. Hitleroski.
   B. Schicklgruber.
   D. Eichmann.

2. The very first bomb dropped by the Allies on Berlin during World War II killed only:
   A. Hitler's brother.
   C. An elephant in the Berlin Zoo.
   B. A British prisoner of war.
   D. The Kaiser's dog named "Uncle Sam."

3. Which of the following did British pilots always carry with them when they went on a mission?
   A. Playing cards
   C. Weapons
   B. Rations
   D. A picture of the queen

4. A secret that American President Franklin Delano Roosevelt tried to keep from the public was that:
   A. He had married a distant cousin.
   C. He smoked.
   B. He was paralyzed from the waist down.
   D. He listened to soap operas on radio.

5. During World War II, Japanese-American men were:
   A. Not permitted to serve in the military.
   C. Permitted to serve as noncombatants.
   B. Permitted to serve in the military.
   D. Permitted to serve only as interpreters.

6. During World War II, when the U.S. Navy wanted to calculate where enemy submarines might surface, they used:
   A. A primitive computer.
   C. Past actions of enemy subs.
   B. A chess player.
   D. The hidden Bible code.

7. A few weeks before the invasion of Normandy, top-secret code words revealing information about the invasion appeared in a:
   A. Speech by Winston Churchill.
   C. Crossword puzzle in a London paper.
   B. Comic book.
   D. Fortune cookie in Tokyo.

Name: _____    Date: _____

8. Before the invasion of Italy, the United States asked for help from:
    A. A Mafia boss in prison.              B. The Pope.
    C. Mussolini's daughter.                D. Michelangelo.

9. The expression "the whole nine yards" comes from WW II. It refers to the length:
    A. Covered in one day at Iwo Jima.      B. Material used to make one uniform.
    C. Of ammunition belts.                 D. Of a P.T. boat.

10. The weapons produced by the 603rd Engineers were unique because they:
    A. Were made of rubber.                 B. Had the highest success rate.
    C. Used experimental weapons.           D. Were handmade.

11. The super Japanese aircraft carrier *Shinano* was called the unperishable castle of the sea.
    It became famous when it:
    A. Sank the *Indianapolis.*             B. Led the attack at Pearl Harbor.
    C. Was sunk on its first voyage.        D. Was converted into a cruise ship.

12. The surprise attack on Pearl Harbor was predicted by:
    A. Nostradamus.                         B. A book in 1925.
    C. Benjamin Franklin in a dream.        D. Three peasant children in Budapest.

13. Hitler did not do well in academic classes in school, so he decided to go to Vienna in order
    to become:
    A. A soldier.                           B. A pastry cook.
    C. An artist.                           D. A ballet dancer.

14. At one time during the War, the army and navy considered putting bombs on:
    A. Bats.                                B. Porpoises.
    C. Kites.                               D. Surfboards.

15. Paul W. Tibbetts piloted the B-29 bomber that dropped the atomic bomb over Hiroshima,
    Japan, on August 6, 1945. The bomber was named *Enola Gay* after:
    A. The first child to die at Pearl Harbor.   B. A sled he had as a child.
    C. His girlfriend.                           D. His mother.

16. The first nuclear weapon used in warfare was called _____. It exploded approxi-
    mately 1,800 feet over Hiroshima, Japan, on the morning of August 6, 1945. The second
    nuclear weapon used in warfare was called _____. It was dropped on Nagasaki,
    Japan, on August 9, 1945.
    A. Abbott, Costello                     B. Little Boy, Fat Man
    C. Adam, Eve                            D. Rising Sun, Setting Sun

Name: _____ Date: _____

17. In the 1940s, there was a beautiful actress named Hedy Lamarr. Among other roles, she played Delilah in the hit movie, *Samson and Delilah.* During World War II, she and a composer whose name was George Antheil contributed to the war effort by:
    A. Inventing a torpedo guidance system.   B. Creating a song about giving blood.
    C. Performing shows on the front lines.   D. Volunteering as nurses.

18. Perhaps the most successful secret code used by American troops was:
    A. Pig Latin.                             B. Navajo Indian language.
    C. Egyptian Hieroglyphics.                D. A code developed during the Civil War.

19. During World War II the original copies of the U.S. Constitution and the Declaration of Independence were:
    A. Laminated.                             B. Stored in Fort Knox, Kentucky.
    C. Stored in a Swiss Bank.                D. Stored at the North Pole.

20. In 1957, the United States dropped a hydrogen bomb in:
    A. Russia.                                B. Italy.
    C. New Mexico.                            D. Atlantis.

21. It is a little known fact that during World War II, Japan:
    A. Bombed the United States.              B. Refused to fight on Saturdays.
    C. Mainly used American-made weapons.     D. Prohibited all talk about the war.

22. Desmond Doss was a conscientious objector. This meant that he was against war and refused to fight in WW II. He was eventually:
    A. Executed.                              B. Given the Medal of Honor.
    C. Sentenced to prison.                   D. Deported.

23. Although Franklin Roosevelt had been president for several years, at the time his mother died in 1941, he had never been permitted to:
    A. Smoke in her presence.                 B. Call her "Mommy."
    C. Attend family reunions.                D. Manage the family money.

24. When President Franklin Delano Roosevelt was a boy, President Cleveland told him, "Franklin:
    A. You're not related to Teddy, are you?"  B. Drop the middle name. It's strange."
    C. I hope you never become president."     D. You should run for office someday."

25. When Douglas MacArthur, the famous general in World War II, attended West Point:
    A. He flunked out.                        B. His mother went with him.
    C. He was expelled for practical jokes.   D. He was an assistant chaplain.

# World War II—Answer Sheet

1.  **B.  Schicklgruber.** Adolf Hitler was the son of Alois and Klara Hitler. Alois's parents were not married so he used his mother's name, Schicklgruber, until 1876; he then adopted the name Hitler.

2.  **C.  An elephant in the Berlin Zoo.**

3.  **A.  Playing cards.** But these were not ordinary playing cards. When these cards were soaked in water, they could be unfolded and would become a map for escape.

4.  **B.  He was paralyzed from the waist down.** In the summer of 1921, he contracted poliomyelitis. While children are vaccinated for this disease today, in 1921 it was disease that could kill, cripple or cause a person to remain in a machine called an "iron lung" for the rest of his life. Franklin recovered, but he remained paralyzed. That fact was hidden from the public as much as possible. He wore braces, and in pictures he was often shown standing.

5.  **B.  Permitted to serve in the military.** One of the most decorated units in U.S. military history was formed primarily by enlistees from the U.S. concentration camps for Japanese-Americans. Although many Japanese-Americans were forced to live in the camps during World War II, some wanted to prove they were really patriotic to the United States. Their unit was nicknamed the Go For Broke Brigade and the Purple Heart Battalion.

6.  **B.  A chess player.** The U.S. Navy had a world champion chess player, Reuben Fine, use his skill as a chess player in order to figure the most logical place where enemy submarines might surface.

7.  **C.  Crossword puzzle in a London paper.** Five weeks before the invasion of Normandy, the London's Daily Telegraph newspaper published five crossword puzzles containing top-secret code words for the invasion of Normandy as the answers to the puzzle. The code words were *Neptune, Mulberry, Utah,* and *Omaha.* Just four days before the invasion, another puzzle solution used the word *Overlord,* which was the code name for the entire Normandy invasion. Scotland Yard investigated, but it turned out to be just a coincidence.

8.  **A.  A Mafia boss in prison.** During World War II the Navy enlisted the help of "Lucky" Luciano, imprisoned Mafia boss, to help with the invasion of Italy. His contacts with the Italian Mafia were invaluable. The Italian Mafia cooperated with America because they didn't like the Fascist government either. They stole maps, documents, and other information for the Allies. They even helped guide the advance units. It was reported that Luciano was never promised anything for his help, but right after the war he was released from prison and deported to Italy.

9.  **C.  Of ammunition belts.** Ammo belts were 27 feet long, so if you used your entire ammo belt on a target, you gave it "the whole nine yards."

10. **A.  Were made of rubber.** Hollywood set designers and fashion designers made rubber tanks, planes, and other weapons to fool the enemy in World War II. There were 1,800 men in the unit, and they would inflate their fake weapons, change insignias, and amplify sounds of machinery in order to fool the Germans into believing that entire divisions were present.

11. **C.  Was sunk on its first voyage.**

# World War II—Answer Sheet

12.  **B.**  **A book in 1925.** Published in 1925, *The Great Pacific War* was written by Hector C. Bywater, a British naval intelligence agent. It outlined a plan that the Japanese might use to fight a war with America. He predicted that the war would begin with a sneak attack on America's naval forces. He did think, though, that the attack would be at Manila Bay rather than Pearl Harbor. Otherwise, his predictions were very accurate.

13.  **C.**  **Artist.** Hitler went to Vienna in 1907 but was unable to gain admission to the Academy of Fine Arts.

14.  **A.**  **Bats.** During World War II, the army and navy studied the possibility of putting bombs on bats and dropping them in Japan. The idea was to catch thousands of bats and store them in freezers so they would sleep. One-ounce incendiary bombs would be attached to them; they would then be dropped from planes. The bats would wake up and fly to hide in buildings. When they chewed the bombs off, the bombs would be detonated causing fires throughout the city. There were experiments with the plan, which were not completely successful. At about the same time, the military turned most of its efforts to developing the atom bomb.

15.  **D.**  **His mother.**

16.  **B.**  **Little Boy, Fat Man.**

17.  **A.**  **Inventing a torpedo guidance system.** They invented and were given a patent for a radio-controlled torpedo guidance system.

18.  **B.**  **Navajo Indian language.** Navajo is a complex, unwritten language. It has no alphabet and is only spoken on Navajo land in America. During World War II it was estimated that only about 30 people who were not Navajo could speak the language. None of these people were Japanese. To make the code even more difficult, the Navajo language was then written in code so that even a native-speaking Navajo Indian could not understand it.

19.  **B.**  **Stored in Fort Knox, Kentucky.**

20.  **C.**  **New Mexico.** Hundreds of times more powerful than the bomb that was set off in Hiroshima, the bomb dropped out of the bomb-bay door and fell from a plane because a safety-release lever was not set correctly. Although the bomb created a 25-foot crater in the desert, it did not explode.

21.  **A.**  **Bombed the United States.** The Japanese sent hundreds of giant rice-paper balloons in the air. Each balloon contained an incendiary bomb. The gas-filled balloons floated over the Pacific Ocean and were supposed to land in the United States and cause fires. Most of the bombs were lost over the ocean, but one exploded in Oregon and killed six people who were on a picnic.

This was not the only attack on the United States during World War II. The Japanese attacked an oil refinery in Southern California in 1942. The refinery was hit by 13 shells fired from a Japanese submarine. It caused damage to the oil well. Also in 1942, the harbor defenses of the Columbia River in Washington state were shelled by a Japanese submarine. The next day, the military depot at Fort Stevens, Oregon, was shelled. Japanese warplanes launched from a submarine dropped bombs several times in Oregon and sank tankers off the coast. In 1944, a German reconnaissance aircraft flew over New York City and took pictures of possible bombing targets.

# World War II—Answer Sheet

22.  **B.**  **Given the Medal of Honor.** Desmond Doss was a conscientious objector because of his religion; he was a Seventh-Day Adventist. However, his religion did not forbid him to work as a medic or go into battle to help the wounded. He was wounded twice while tending to wounded soldiers on the front line. He once crawled into a cave filled with Japanese snipers in order to administer plasma to a wounded American. Another time he was ordered to leave an area because it was too dangerous, but instead he rescued 75 wounded Americans. For his bravery, Doss received the Medal of Honor from President Harry Truman.

23.  **D.**  **Manage the family money.** Although Franklin was president and had presided over eight annual budgets of the United States, Sara Delano Roosevelt did not trust her son to manage the family money because she did not think he was responsible enough.

24.  **C.**  **I hope you never become president.”**

25.  **B.**  **His mother went with him.** She rented an apartment that had a view of Douglas's dormitory room. She wanted to be sure that he studied.

Name: _____ Date: _____

# Franklin Delano Roosevelt Quotation

| O | H | F | E | E | O | A | N | R | L |

Left side (top to bottom): T T B E F V L A

Right side (top to bottom): I Y S T F H E I A

| E | H | S | E | T | W | I | G | R | N |

Franklin Delano Roosevelt, the thirty-second President of the United States, became president during the Great Depression and brought hope to Americans as he developed many new programs to help the economy and the people. He eventually was reelected three more times, making him the only president ever to be elected to four terms.

Under his leadership, the role of government was greatly expanded. Programs such as Social Security and Unemployment Insurance were implemented. National laws ending child labor, establishing a minimum wage, and limiting the maximum hours of labor were also passed.

His legacy includes leadership during two of the most critical and difficult times the United States ever faced, the Great Depression and World War II. Roosevelt brought leadership and instilled confidence and hope in the people of the United States.

One quote for which he will always be remembered was delivered in his first inaugural address. The quote was made about the Depression, but it also inspired Americans during World War II. Do you know what the quote was? It is hidden in the frame around Roosevelt's picture shown above. To discover the quote, you must go around the frame twice, reading every *other* letter. Where do you start and which way do you read around the frame? That's what you have to figure out. Write the answer on the lines provided.

Name: _____ Date: _____

# Lincoln and Kennedy

Many have noticed the similarities in the lives and the assassinations of Presidents Abraham Lincoln and John F. Kennedy. We realize that the similarities are just a coincidence, but they are interesting and even a bit bizarre. Fill in the blanks below and see if you don't agree.

1. a. Abraham Lincoln was elected to Congress in (Year) _____.
   b. John F. Kennedy was elected to Congress in (Year) _____.
2. a The name "Lincoln" contains (Number) _____ letters.
   b. The name "Kennedy" contains (Number) _____ letters.
3. a. Lincoln was concerned with civil rights.
   b. Kennedy was concerned with _____.
4. a. Lincoln was involved in a series of debates.
   b. Kennedy was involved in a series of _____.
5. a. Lincoln was elected President in (Year) _____.
   b. Kennedy was elected President in (Year) _____.
6. a. Lincoln won the election with less than 50 percent of the vote.
   b. Kennedy won the election with less than _____ of the vote.
7. a. Lincoln lost a child while living in the White House.
   b. Kennedy lost a child while living in the _____.
8. a. Lincoln had a secretary named _____.
   b. Kennedy had a secretary named _____.
9. a. Lincoln considered not going to the theater where he was assassinated.
   b. Kennedy considered not going to _____ where he was assassinated.
10. a. Lincoln was shot in the back of the head.
    b. Kennedy was shot _____.
11. a. Lincoln was shot on (Day of the week) _____.
    b. Kennedy was shot on (Day of the week) _____.
12. a. Lincoln was with his wife when he was assassinated.
    b. Kennedy was with _____ when he was assassinated.
13. a. Lincoln was shot in (Name) _____ Theater.
    b. Kennedy was shot in a _____ car, made by the _____ Motor Company.
14. a. Lincoln's assassin was known by (Number)_____ names.
    b. Kennedy's assassin was known by (Number)_____ names.
15. a. Lincoln was assassinated by John Wilkes Booth, a Southerner.
    b. Kennedy was assassinated by Lee Harvey Oswald, a _____.
16. a. Lincoln's assassin's name has (Number) _____ letters.
    b. Kennedy's assassin's name has (Number) _____ letters.
17. a Booth ran from a _____ and was caught in a _____.
    b. Oswald ran from a _____ and was caught in a _____.
18. a. Booth was assassinated before his trial.
    b. Oswald was assassinated before his _____.
19. a. Lincoln was succeeded by a Southerner named _____.
    b. Kennedy was succeeded by a _____ named _____.
20. a. Andrew Johnson, who succeeded Lincoln, was born in (Year) _____.
    b. Lyndon Johnson, who succeeded Kennedy, was born in (Year) _____.

Name:_____ Date:_____

# American Presidents

The President of the United States is the most powerful position in America and, some think, the most powerful in the world. Over the years, many different kinds of people have served in this position—wealthy, poor, successful, and failures. Some presidents have been very unusual and might even be considered peculiar.

Read each of the following unusual facts about American presidents and circle the letter before the correct answer.

1. Andrew Johnson and Millard Fillmore are unusual because they were:
   A. Married to sisters.              B. Indentured servants.
   C. Impeached.                      D. Sons of state governors.

2. Which one of the following had the *same* birth name as the one he used as President?
   A. Rutherford B. Hayes             B. Ulysses S. Grant
   C. Gerald Ford                     D. William Clinton

3. When John Quincy Adams was president, he liked to do this at the Potomac River.
   A. Fish                            B. Ice skate
   C. See if he could throw a dollar across    D. Skinny-dip

4. When John Tyler was told that President Harrison had died and that he had become president, Tyler was:
   A. On vacation in France           B. Playing marbles
   C. Attending the funeral of Harrison's son    D. Working to impeach Harrison

5. When Vice President Martin Van Buren presided over the Senate he wore:
   A. A stovepipe hat.                B. Two pistols.
   C. A pin that said "Kiss me, I'm Irish."    D. A purple vest.

6. David Rice Atchison became part of American history because he was:
   A. President for a day.            B. The first secretary of state.
   C. The realtor who listed Louisiana.    D. Washington's dentist.

7. When the Whig Party nominated Zachary Taylor as their presidential candidate, they sent him a letter informing him, but he didn't find out for a month because:
   A. Of a letter carrier's strike.    B. The Pony Express rider was killed.
   C. It was sent to the wrong address.    D. He refused to pay the postage due.

8. The only bachelor president was:
   A. Millard Fillmore.               B. Woodrow Wilson.
   C. James Buchanan.                 D. Zachary Taylor.

Name: _____ Date: _____

9.  William Henry Harrison was killed by:
    A. An assassin.                          B. Lightning.
    C. His inaugural address.                D. The CIA.

10. Neither Benjamin Harrison nor his wife would:
    A. Eat broccoli.                         B. Ride on a train.
    C. Speak to their servants.              D. Turn the lights on or off.

11. When President Hoover and his wife wanted to speak privately, they spoke in:
    A. A closet.                             B. Pig Latin.
    C. Sign language.                        D. Chinese.

12. President Cleveland was the only president to:
    A. Resign.                               B. Have been divorced.
    C. Marry his cousin.                     D. Win nonconsecutive terms.

13. Grover Cleveland had:
    A. A jaw made of rubber.                 B. A pet monkey named "Tony."
    C. A sister who married Teddy Roosevelt. D. A golden pass to the Ringling Circus.

14. Many people feel that Millard Fillmore's greatest accomplishment as President of the United
    States was to negotiate a treaty with Peru over the use of:
    A. Coffee.                               B. Oil.
    C. The Panama Canal.                     D. Bird droppings.

15. President Andrew Johnson:
    A. Was a cobbler by trade.               B. Would only eat the vegetables he grew.
    C. Made all of his own clothes.          D. Had a foot race against a horse.

16. James Garfield was able to write in Greek while he:
    A. Wrote in Latin with the other hand.   B. Whistled Dixie.
    C. Spoke in French.                      D. Dictated to his secretary in English.

17. When President Cleveland's wife was a baby:
    A. Cleveland bought her a baby carriage.  B. She could walk at six months of age.
    C. She and Cleveland shared a nanny.      D. She was deaf until age nine.

18. The presidential campaign of 1912 was notable because:
    A. Three presidents ran.                  B. It had no vice-presidential candidates.
    C. It was the first time women could vote. D. Theodore Roosevelt ran unopposed.

# American Presidents—Answer Sheet

1. **B.** **Indentured servants.** In the early part of the nineteenth century, many poor white families in the South sold their young children into servitude. They were known as indentured servants. A man would pay the parents of a child a certain amount; it then became the responsibility of the man to care for and feed the young child. He would also teach the child a trade. Andrew Johnson was 12 years old when he became an indentured servant. After a few years, he ran away. Millard Fillmore was also an indentured servant; however, he purchased his freedom for $30.

2. **A.** **Rutherford B. Hayes.** Gerald Ford was originally Leslie L. King, and William Clinton's last name was Blythe. In both cases the names were changed as a result of adoptions by their stepfathers. Ulysses S. Grant's first and middle name were not Ulysses and Simpson. His full name was actually Hiram Ulysses Grant. The congressman who sponsored Grant to West Point dropped the name of Hiram and added Simpson, which was Grant's mother's maiden name. It is not known why he changed Grant's name when he registered him at West Point. Many feel that the reason was that "Hiram" does not sound military enough.

3. **D.** **Skinny-dip.** John Quincy Adams would swim in the Potomac without his clothes. On one occasion while he was swimming, someone stole his clothes and Adams had to ask a young boy who was passing by to run back to the White House and get him some clothes to wear.

4. **B.** **Playing marbles.**

5. **B.** **Two pistols.** This was protection from frequent violence.

6. **A.** **President for a day.** Atchison was President Pro Tempore of the Senate on March 4, 1849, the day President James K. Polk's term expired at noon. Zachary Taylor, the president-elect, refused to take the oath of office on March 4 because it was Sunday. Ordinarily the vice president would become president, but Polk's vice president had resigned a few days before. So, according to law, Atchison was president for one day until Taylor took his oath.

7. **D.** **He refused to pay the postage due.** The letter the Whig party sent notifying Taylor of the nomination carried no postage. When it was sent to Taylor's home, he refused to pay 10 cents postage due; so the letter was sent to the dead letter office. It was not until the following month that the Whig Party sent him a prepaid letter and Taylor learned that he was the Whig candidate.

8. **C.** **James Buchanan.**

9. **C.** **His inaugural address.** He gave a very long inaugural address on a very cold winter's day. He spoke for two hours. He didn't have a hat, coat, or gloves, and he was 68 years old. He caught pneumonia and died a month later. He delivered the longest inaugural address of any president and served the shortest time.

10. **D.** **Turn the lights on or off.** Both Harrison and his wife were so afraid of electricity that they would not turn the lights on or off. They had the servants do it.

11. **D.** **Chinese.**

# American Presidents—Answer Sheet

**12. D.** **Win nonconsecutive terms.** Grover Cleveland barely won the election in 1884, and four years later he received more than a hundred thousand votes than his opponent, Benjamin Harrison. However, Cleveland lost the Electoral College vote, so he was not elected. In 1892, however, he was reelected. Since he served two terms, many people have trouble deciding how many presidents we've had. In other words, should Cleveland just be considered the twenty-second president or was he the twenty-second as well as the twenty-fourth president?

**13. A.** **A jaw made of rubber.** Grover Cleveland had cancer in the roof of his mouth. Part of his jaw was cut out, but he made a quick recovery. Cleveland did not want the public to know that he was ill. He was afraid that if the public found out, there might be a financial crisis, so he had an artificial jaw made out of vulcanized rubber to hide the fact that he had had surgery.

**14. D.** **Bird droppings.** Actually, it was called guano. Guano is the accumulated deposits of the dried droppings of seabirds and bats that has been used for fertilizer in parts of South America. In the nineteenth-century, guano exporters bagged the substance from the coastal islands near Peru. It was shipped to Europe and America. The development of artificial fertilizers, for the most part, minimized the importance of guano in the early twentieth century.

**15. C.** **Made all of his own clothes.** Andrew Johnson was a tailor. When Andrew Johnson was governor of Tennessee, he made a suit for the governor of Kentucky. Johnson never went to school. He learned the alphabet while working in a tailor shop. He taught himself to read and his girlfriend taught him to write.

**16. A.** **Wrote in Latin with the other hand.** James Garfield was able to write Greek with one hand and Latin with the other hand at the same time. Garfield also spoke German so well that he is the only president to have campaigned in German.

**17. A.** **Cleveland bought her a baby carriage.** Cleveland had known his wife since the day she was born. She was his former law partner's daughter. Cleveland had become her legal guardian when she was 11 years old. When they were married, he was 49 and she was 21. He was the only president to be married in the White House.

**18. A.** **Three presidents ran against each other.** The presidential campaign of 1912 was the only election in history where three presidents ran against each other—Theodore Roosevelt, William Howard Taft, and Woodrow Wilson.

Name:_____ Date:_____

# Presidential Vanity License Plates

Vanity licence plates for automobiles are very popular today. A vanity license plate is one an owner chooses that tells something about him or her. When a person reads the plate aloud, one can discover something about the car owner's interests or concerns. While vanity plates are a recent development, what vanity plates do you think would be appropriate for some of our former presidents? Given below are some suggestions. See if you can figure out for which president each plate might be the most appropriate. Write your answer under each plate.

| **PAPA USA** USA | **MNSP8TR** USA | **LUZINA BYR** USA |
|---|---|---|
| 1._____ | 2._____ | 3._____ |
| **OLD HKRE** USA | **IKE** USA | **PNUT 4MR** USA |
| 4._____ | 5._____ | 6._____ |
| **4TM PREZ** USA | **PT 109** USA | **TDE BR** USA |
| 7._____ | 8._____ | 9._____ |
| **1ST ADMZ** USA | **AKTR** USA | **4D** USA |
| 10._____ | 11._____ | 12._____ |
| **H20 G8** USA | **2ND MPCHD** USA | **KWNSI** USA |
| 13._____ | 14._____ | 15._____ |

Name: _____ Date: _____

# US

The letters "US" are very important to our country. Everyone knows that they are the initials that represent the name of the United States of America. These two letters are also found in many words that are important in our country's history. Using the clues below, fill in the correct word or words. Each of the answers includes the letters "US."

1. Many people give this Italian explorer credit for discovering America in 1492.
   ___ ___ ___ ___ ___ ___ U  S ___

2. The result of the discovery of this precious metal in California is called the...
   ___ ___ ___ ___   ___ U  S ___

3. The Latin motto meaning "from many, one" appears on all U.S. coins.
   ___   ___ ___ ___ ___ ___ ___ U  S   ___ ___ ___ ___

4. This phrase in English also appears on U.S. money
   ___ ___   ___ ___ ___   ___ ___   ___ ___ U  S ___

5. He developed a mechanical reaper in 1831.
   ___ ___ ___ U  S ___   ___ ___ ___ ___ ___ ___ ___ ___

6. Has was elected the 41st President of the United States in 1988.
   ___ ___ ___ ___ ___ ___   ___ U  S ___

7. He was the 18th President of the United States and a famous Union general in the Civil War.
   U  S ___   ___ ___ ___ ___ ___

8. This is a New England state. Its capital is Boston.
   ___ ___ ___ ___ ___ ___ ___ ___ U  S ___ ___ ___ ___

9. This, along with "liberty," is recited in the last phrase of the *Pledge of Allegiance.*
   ___ U  S ___ ___ ___ ___ ___

10. An official count of U.S. citizens that takes place every ten years.
    ___ ___ ___ ___ U  S

11. A large-caliber firearm used during colonial times.
    ___ U  S ___ ___ ___

12. Rosa Parks refused to give up her seat on this in the 1950s.
    ___ U  S

13. An American cavalry officer defeated at the Battle of the Little Bighorn.
    ___ U  S ___ ___ ___

14. The oldest city in the United States. It is in northeastern Florida.
    ___ ___   ___ ___ ___ U  S ___ ___ ___ ___

15. We bought Alaska from this country.
    ___ U  S ___ ___ ___

Name: _____ Date: _____

# Famous American Vehicles

Throughout American history, there have been many vehicles that have become famous. Some of them are listed below. Under the heading, "Kind," identify the kind of vehicle. Under the heading "Description," write specific information to identify the vehicle. The first vehicle is given as an example.

| Name of Vehicle | Kind of Vehicle | Description |
|---|---|---|
| Nelson | Horse | George Washington's Horse |
| Pueblo | | |
| Titanic | | |
| Sultana | | |
| Lusitania | | |
| Hindenburg | | |
| Apollo 11 (Columbia) | | |
| Flyer I | | |
| Enola Gay | | |
| Missouri | | |
| Arizona | | |
| Monitor | | |
| Merrimack | | |
| Constitution | | |
| Traveler | | |
| Spirit of St. Louis | | |
| Mayflower | | |
| Niña | | |

Name: _____ Date: _____

# U.S. Landmarks

There are many landmarks and structures in the United States that mark an important event in America's history or have historical significance. Listed below are some unusual facts concerning some of these landmarks. Read each of the following sentences and circle the letter before the correct answer.

1. The famous London Bridge over the River Thames, built in the 1830s, is now located in:
   A. London.
   B. Las Vegas.
   C. Disney World.
   D. Lake Havasu City, Arizona.

2. Compared to Boulder Dam, Hoover Dam is:
   A. Taller.
   B. Older.
   C. Longer.
   D. The same.

3. The top of the Empire State Building was originally intended as a:
   A. Mooring place for dirigibles.
   B. Place to sunbathe.
   C. Pad for helicopters.
   D. Astronomical observation deck.

4. The "Hollywood" sign in Hollywood, California, was first built in 1923. It was originally:
   A. A sign for a funeral home.
   B. A real estate ad.
   C. A sign for a theme park.
   D. A sign for a plant nursery.

5. The world's first national park was:
   A. Disney World.
   B. Grand Canyon.
   C. Yellowstone.
   D. Niagara Falls.

6. The only mobile national monuments are:
   A. Hanson Cabs in New York.
   B. San Francisco cable cars.
   C. The Wright Brothers' planes.
   D. The Goodyear blimps.

7. What is the original name of the statue that sits in New York harbor?
   A. The Statue of Liberty.
   B. Liberty Enlightening the World.
   C. Lady With a Torch.
   D. Miss Liberty.

8. The Pentagon has 284 of these.
   A. Offices
   B. Telephones
   C. Photocopy machines
   D. Rest rooms

9. Alcatraz prison in San Francisco was first used as a prison by the U.S. Army during the:
   A. War with Mexico.
   B. Civil War.
   C. Japanese interment.
   D. Indian Wars.

Name: _____ Date: _____

10. Many people want to visit the Empire State Building in order to:
    A. Get married.                    B. Feed the pigeons.
    C. Drop water balloons.            D. Slide down the bannister.

11. On a clear day, you can see five states from the top of the Empire State Building in New York City. Which one of the following states can you *not* see?
    A. Rhode Island                    B. Massachusetts
    C. Pennsylvania                    D. New Jersey

12. The cost to build the Erie Canal was paid not only by tolls on the canal, but was also financed by a tax on:
    A. Bubble gum.                     B. Salt.
    C. Cigarettes.                     D. Bicycles.

13. The index finger of the Statue of Liberty is:
    A. One foot long.                  B. Four feet long.
    C. Eight feet long.                D. Twenty feet long.

14. In downtown Enterprise, Alabama, there is a statue honoring:
    A. Dolly Parton.                   B. The boll weevil.
    C. Robert E. Lee.                  D. Elvis Presley.

15. The Brooklyn Bridge, completed in 1883, was the first great suspension bridge in the United States that had cables formed from parallel steel wires that were spun in place. At first people were afraid to cross this strange and dangerous-looking bridge. In an effort to convince New Yorkers that the Brooklyn Bridge was safe for pedestrians:
    A. Tanks were driven across it.    B. Elephants were led across it.
    C. Ten Sumo wrestlers rode bikes over it.    D. The mayor drove a truck across it.

16. Broadway is a famous street in New York that is known as a center of the entertainment industry. What was the original use of Broadway?
    A. Buffalo walk                    B. Indian warpath
    C. City market                     D. Slave market

17. In Washington D.C., no building may be built taller than:
    A. The Lincoln Memorial.           B. The White House.
    C. The flag on the Capitol.        D. The Washington Monument.

18. The White House has been known as the "President's Palace," the "Executive Mansion," or sometimes simply the "President's House." Who officially gave the White House its current name?
    A. Dolley Madison                  B. Theodore Roosevelt
    C. Ronald Reagan                   D. P.T. Barnum

# U.S. Landmarks—Answer Sheet

1. **D.** **Lake Havasu City, Arizona.** London Bridge, which stretched over the River Thames for almost 140 years, was sinking. In 1968, it was sold it to Robert P. McCulloch for $2.6 million. McCulloch used the bridge to connect Lake Havasu City to an island in the lake. It took three years and more than $7 million to dismantle, pack, ship, and rebuild the bridge in Lake Havasu City.

2. **D.** **The same.** It is the same dam. It was originally called Boulder Dam but was renamed for former President Hoover in 1947.

3. **A.** **Mooring place for dirigibles.** Built in 1930–31 on Fifth Avenue in New York City, it was the tallest building in the world until 1971, when the first tower of the World Trade Center was finished. The building was opened during the Depression, and the owners had difficulty in renting the space. Consequently, revenues from sightseers were used to cover costs.

4. **B.** **A real estate ad.** Fifty feet tall and 450 feet across, the sign was first erected in 1923 and read: Hollywoodland. Hollywood, California, was mainly a farming community.

5. **C.** **Yellowstone.** Located in eastern Idaho, southern Montana, and northwestern Wyoming, Yellowstone National Park was dedicated in 1872.

6. **B.** **San Francisco cable cars.**

7. **B.** **Liberty Enlightening the World.**

8. **D.** **Rest rooms.**

9. **B.** **Civil War.**

10. **A.** **Get married.** Many consider the Empire State Building to be one of the most romantic places to be married. On Valentine's Day, those who are married on the eightieth floor of the building become members of the Empire State Building Wedding Club and will have free admission to the observatories on their anniversaries.

11. **A.** **Rhode Island.**

12. **B.** **Salt.** The Erie Canal, which connects New York City, via the Hudson River, with Lake Erie at Buffalo, New York, was financed with a tax of 12.5 percent on New York State salt. The tax paid for nearly half of the $7 million construction cost.

13. **C.** **Eight feet long.** The Statue of Liberty measures 35 feet in diameter at the waist and has a fingernail that measures 10 by 13 inches. The Statue's mouth is 3 feet wide.

14. **B.** **The boll weevil.** Farmers in this area raised cotton almost exclusively. When the Mexican boll weevil arrived in the United States, it caused a great deal of damage to the cotton crop and hurt the prosperity of the area. In 1915 there was a disastrous infestation of the weevil. It destroyed one-third of the harvest. From that point on, farmers realized they should not rely on one crop alone. They began planting peanuts, potatoes, corn, hay, and sugar cane. They became more prosperous than ever before. They were grateful to the weevil.

15. **B.** **Elephants were led across it.** Circus owner P.T. Barnum led 21 of his elephants across it.

16. **B.** **Indian warpath.**

17 **D.** **The Washington Monument.**

18. **B.** **Theodore Roosevelt.**

Name: _____    Date: _____

# Sports

Sports have always been an important part of the daily life of Americans. The colonists in New England were not as interested in sports and other forms of entertainment as those in the other colonies. However, colonists in the Southern colonies were very ardent sportsmen. Over the years, American's interest and participation in sports has grown tremendously. Today we are not only able to engage in sports, but in the convenience of our own homes, we are also able to watch and enjoy world-class athletes participate in games on television.

Along with the growth of sports, there have been many interesting situations and occurrences of which most people are unaware. Listed below are some examples of these. Read each of the following sentences and circle the letter before the correct answer.

1.  Seventeen-year-old Virne Beatrice "Jackie" Mitchell is the only woman to ever:
    A. Run a mile in under four minutes.        B. Play for a major college football team.
    C. Strike out Babe Ruth and Lou Gehrig.    D. Knock out Muhammad Ali.

2.  President Abraham Lincoln's favorite sport was:
    A. Wrestling.                               B. Baseball.
    C. Fox hunting.                             D. Horse racing.

3.  In 1930, Fred P. Newton swam the Mississippi:
    A. While pulling a barge.                   B. Underwater.
    C. Lengthwise.                              D. On his back.

4.  The costliest sport due to injuries in the U.S (including medical, legal, and other costs) is:
    A. Bicycling.                               B. Football.
    C. Skydiving.                               D. Skateboarding.

5.  Pete Gray was the only major league baseball player:
    A. To play for seven teams.                 B. To pitch with either hand.
    C. Never to appear on a baseball card.      D. With one arm.

6.  The oldest individual to win a medal in the Olympics was:
    A. Fifty-two years old.                     B. Sixty-two years old.
    C. Seventy-two years old.                   D. Eighty-two years old.

7.  Eddie Gaedel was the only major league baseball player who:
    A. Was a midget.                            B. Was legally blind.
    C. Won an Olympic medal for boxing.         D. Was also an opera singer.

8.  For the first time, the play-by-play of Super Bowl XXX in 1996 was broadcast in:
    A. French.                                  B. Navajo.
    C. China.                                   D. Esperanto.

112

Name: _____     Date: _____

9.  Before 1859, baseball umpires:
    A. Stood 20 feet behind the catcher.        B. Sat in rocking chairs.
    C. Had to be at least 40 years old.         D. Did not exist.

10. After Mike Tyson bit the ear of Evander Holyfield during a heavyweight boxing match, the
    Hollywood Wax Museum moved Tyson's figure:
    A. Out of the museum.                        B. Into storage.
    C. Into the candle factory.                  D. Next to the figure of a cannibal.

11. In 1931, the Harlem Globetrotters once played before only one person. Who was it?
    A. Adolf Hitler                              B. President Wilson
    C. Pope Pius XI                              D. Winston Churchill

12. The huddle formation used by football teams began at:
    A. Gallaudet University.                     B. Yale.
    C. Harvard.                                  D. Massachusetts Institute of Technology.

13. This event commemorates a 1925 emergency operation to get medical supplies during a
    deadly diphtheria epidemic.
    A. Boston Marathon                           B. Pentathlon
    C. March of Dimes                            D. Iditarod dog sled race

14. The practice of slapping palms—giving the high five—began in:
    A. 1931.                                     B. 1951.
    C. 1971.                                     D. 1991.

15. This sport became so popular in England and Scotland in 1457 that King James II banned
    it because he thought it would hurt national defense. What was it?
    A. Soccer                                    B. Golf
    C. Archery                                   D. Pie-eating contests

16. The largest collection of baseball cards can be found in:
    A. The Metropolitan Museum of Art.           B. The Louvre.
    C. The Baseball Hall of Fame.                D. Bill Gates' closet.

17. In bowling alley slang, a "turkey" refers to:
    A. Someone who loses.                        B. The one who pays for the beer.
    C. A left-handed bowler.                     D. Three strikes in a row.

18. This was an Olympic event from 1900 to 1920.
    A. Tug-of-war                                B. Boomerang toss
    C. Ring toss                                 D. Push-ups

# Sports—Answer Sheet

1. **C.** **Strike out Babe Ruth and Lou Gehrig.** After spring training in 1931, the New York Yankees stopped in Tennessee to play an exhibition game against a minor league team. The pitcher for the minor league team gave up so many hits in the first inning that a relief pitcher, Virne Beatrice "Jackie" Mitchell replaced him. She didn't have much speed, but her breaking ball was hard to hit. The first batter she faced was Babe Ruth, one of the greatest baseball players of all time. She struck him out. The last strike was called, but he didn't swing. The next to face her was Lou Gehrig, another legend of baseball. She struck him out on three straight pitches. In spite of this incredible feat and her obvious talent, she was never called up to the major leagues.

2. **A.** **Wrestling.** He enjoyed wrestling as a participant, not as a spectator. There are several stories of wrestling matches in which Lincoln participated. One well-known wrestling match was one that Lincoln had with a town bully in New Salem, Illinois. The bully's name was Jack Armstrong. Lincoln was taller at 6′, 4″ and 185 pounds. Armstrong was shorter, but powerfully built. Some accounts of the fight say that Lincoln won. In others, the match ended in a draw.

3. **C.** **Lengthwise.** He began his trip near Minneapolis on July 6 and finished at New Orleans on December 29.

4. **A.** **Bicycling.** Much of the cost arises from emergency medical treatment and lawsuits. Sadly, a large percentage of those injuries are head injuries, which can be prevented by wearing helmets.

5. **D.** **With one arm.** While in the minor leagues, he consistently had a batting average at or above .300. He played for the St. Louis Browns major league team in 1945, but only hit .218. In center field when he would catch a ball, he would quickly tuck his glove under the stump of his right shoulder, grab the ball, and throw it into the infield. It was done almost as quickly as if he had two arms.

6. **C.** **Seventy-two.** Oscar Swahn won a silver medal in shooting for Sweden in 1920.

7. **A.** **Was a midget.** On August 19, 1951, the St. Louis Browns' owner, Bill Veck inserted Eddie Gaedel into the starting lineup. No one knew he was on the team and were amazed when a 3′, 7″, 65-pound man stood at the plate to bat. He was wearing the number "$\frac{1}{8}$." When he assumed the batting position, it was estimated that he offered the pitcher an inch and a half strike zone. He walked the first time at bat and was replaced by a pinch runner. Ford Frick, the baseball commissioner, banned Eddie and all other midgets from playing baseball.

8. **B.** **Navajo.** NBC-TV offered a secondary, foreign-language audio feed to its affiliates.

9. **B.** **Sat in rocking chairs.** Umpires were unpaid volunteers in the early days of the sport. Sometimes a spectator was the umpire. At other times the umpire might be a player chosen by the home team with the consent of the rival team's captain. In 1878, the National League of Professional Baseball Clubs decided that home baseball teams should pay umpires $5 per game.

10. **D.** **Next to the figure of a cannibal.** Actually, they moved Mike Tyson's figure into the Chamber of Horrors and placed it next to the figure of Dr. Hannibal Lecter. Lecter is a character from the movie *The Silence of the Lambs*.

11. **C.** **Pope Pius XI.**

# Sports—Answer Sheet

12. **A.** **Gallaudet University.** Gallaudet University is a liberal arts college for deaf people in Washington, D.C. In order to prevent other schools from reading their sign language, they grouped themselves in a huddle.

13. **D.** **Iditarod dog sled race.**

14. **A.** **1931.** In the 1931 Rose Bowl game, a player who would become known as "Five-Yard" Fogerty carried 25 times and gained exactly 5 yards on each carry. During the game his teammates began to celebrate each time Fogerty repeated his feat by slapping palms. The term "high fives" was coined many years later.

15. **B.** **Golf.** King James II thought that golf was taking too much time away from archery practice.

16. **A.** **The Metropolitan Museum of Art.**

17. **D.** **Three strikes in a row.** In the 1800s, around the holidays, the first person to roll three strikes in a row was rewarded with a live turkey. Whenever the first person would roll the first three strikes, his friends would say, "That's a turkey!"

18. **A.** **Tug-of-war.**

Name: _____    Date: _____

# Many Different Hats of America

When someone says that a person wears two different hats, he means that the person has two different jobs or shares his loyalty with two different causes. This phrase probably arose from the fact that many professions or tasks require a special hat. In fact, in many cases you could identify a person's profession by the hat he or she was wearing. Certainly a firefighter or a police officer could easily be identified by their hats. In addition to jobs or occupations, different styles of hats or headgear were worn by different groups and during different periods in our history.

Look at the hats below. They are examples of some of the hats that have been worn throughout the history of America. Can you tell who might have worn them? Use the words given at the bottom of the page and write the correct answer under each hat.

1._____    2._____    3._____    4._____

5._____    6._____    7._____    8._____

9._____    10._____    11._____    12._____

13._____    14._____    15._____    16._____

**Use these words:**

| Abraham Lincoln | astronaut | aviator | Confederate soldier |
|---|---|---|---|
| conquistador | cowboy | marine | Indian chief |
| minuteman | pilgrim | pirate | pioneer woman |
| World War I soldier | trapper | sailor | World War II soldier |

Name: _____ Date: _____

# Scrambled Headlines From the '90s

Shown below are several headlines that appeared in the 1990s. The only problem is, they are mixed up. Each headline has been broken into three parts. Each part is shown in one of three columns. Column two has been scrambled and so has column three. You are to start with the name in column one and then find the correct phrases that complete the headline in column two and column three. All of the phrases from column two stay in column two. The same is true for column three. Write the completed headlines on the lines on page 119. You might want to mark off the phrases as you use them. The first headline is given as an example.

| Column One | Column Two | Column Three |
|---|---|---|
| 1. ~~Timothy McVeigh~~ | becomes youngest figure skater | to win the Masters |
| 2. Madonna | killed 11 students, 2 teachers | to win Olympic gold medal |
| 3. President Zachary Taylor | becomes first nonwhite golfer | in Los Angeles |
| 4. Mike Tyson | gave birth to a daughter | at Columbine High School |
| 5. O.J. Simpson | explodes off Long Island | for mailing bombs |
| 6. Tiger Woods | returned to space | named Lourdes Maria Ciccone |
| 7. Christopher Reeve | was disqualified | but found not guilty |
| 8. D. Klebold and Eric Harris | videotaped beating Rodney King | home run record |
| 9. Flight 800 | ~~was convicted~~ | killing 230 |
| 10. Astronaut John Glenn | was impeached | to see if he was poisoned |
| 11. Mark McGwire | was exhumed | from Michael Jackson |
| 12. Tara Lipinski | was found not guilty | after falling off a horse |
| 13. Los Angeles police | broke single-season | of murdering his former wife |
| 14. President Clinton | files for divorce | ~~of the Oklahoma City bombing~~ |
| 15. Lisa Marie Presley | was arrested | after biting off Holyfield's ear |
| 16. Unabomber Ted Kaczynski | was paralyzed | aboard the shuttle Discovery |

117

Name:_____ Date:_____

# Scrambled Headlines From the '90s

Write the completed headlines from page 118 on the lines below. The first one has been done for you.

| Column One | Column Two | Column Three |
|---|---|---|
| 1. *Timothy McVeigh* | *was convicted* | *of the Oklahoma City bombing* |
| 2. | | |
| 3. | | |
| 4. | | |
| 5. | | |
| 6. | | |
| 7. | | |
| 8. | | |
| 9. | | |
| 10. | | |
| 11. | | |
| 12. | | |
| 13. | | |
| 14. | | |
| 15. | | |
| 16. | | |

# Answer Keys to Activities

**A Mystery from History: Columbus and the Mystery of the Disappearing Moon (page 7)**
By consulting astronomical charts and books, Columbus was able to predict a lunar eclipse. Columbus and his men were eventually rescued and returned to Spain.

**Explorers Puzzle (page 11)**
1. DESOTO
2. CARTIER
3. COLUMBUS
4. CORTEZ
5. CABOT
6. VESPUCCI
7. MAGELLAN
8. PIZARRO
9. DIAZ
10. LASALLE
11. HUDSON
Hidden Message: Discoveries

**Exploration Cube Puzzle (page 12)**
**Hidden Message: Northwest Passage**

**A Mystery From History: The Spanish Gold Mystery (page 13)**
The Spanish explorers used the following method to move everyone across the river:
1. First, two Indians were sent over.
2. One Indian brought back the canoe.
3. The two remaining Indians went over.
4. One of the Indians paddled the canoe back.
5. Two of the Spanish explorers then went over.
6. One of the explorers and one of the Indians then brought the canoe back.
7. The last two explorers then went over. There were then three explorers on the far side of the river with one of the natives. This Indian went back to get the other two natives, one at a time.

**First Thanksgiving Meal Grid (page 20)**

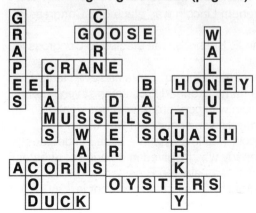

**Thirteen Colonies Puzzle (page 25)**

MASSACHUSETTS
VIRGINIA
RHODE ISLAND
NORTH CAROLINA
GEORGIA
DELAWARE
NEW YORK
NEW HAMPSHIRE
SOUTH CAROLINA
MARYLAND
CONNECTICUT
NEW JERSEY
PENNSYLVANIA

**Sports in the Colonies Logic Problem (pages 26–27)**

| Name | Event | Month | Money Lost |
|------|-------|-------|-----------|
| Andrews | Foot Racing | April | $1 |
| Jameson | Wrestling | February | $2 |
| Gonzales | Horse Racing | January | $5 |
| Henrickson | Rounders | March | $3 |
| Lymenstall | Log Rolling | May | $4 |

**Releasing Slaves Logic Problem (pages 32–33)**

| Name | Job as Slave | Job as Freeman | Month |
|------|-------------|----------------|-------|
| James | Coachman | Cooper | January |
| Thomas | Gardener | Tinker | February |
| Seth | Field hand | Blacksmith | April |
| Andrew | Horse groomer | Farmer | June |
| Henry | Butler | Teamster | August |

**Buying Horses Logic Problem (pages 37–38)**

| Name | Color of Horse | Reason for Buying | Disease/ Injury |
|------|---------------|-------------------|-----------------|
| Lewis | Spotted | Pulling Wagons | Blindness |
| Carver | White | Breeding | Botulism |
| Holmes | Palomino | Recreational Riding | Broken Leg |
| Ogle | Chestnut | Plowing | Tetanus |
| San Martin | Black | Racing | Lame |

**A Revolutionary War Slogan (page 49)**
TAXATION WITHOUT REPRESENTATION IS TYRANNY.

# Answer Keys to Activities

**A Mystery From History: Robert Shurtleff (page 50)**
ROBERT WAS REALLY A WOMAN DISGUISED AS A MAN.

Deborah Sampson was born in 1760 and died in 1827. Sampson was an indentured servant in Middleborough, Massachusetts. At the age of 18, she became legally free and decided to join the army. Since women were not allowed in the military, she disguised herself as a man in order to fight in the Revolutionary War. She used the name Robert Shurtleff when she enlisted in the 4th Massachusetts Regiment. When it was discovered that Deborah was a woman, she was discharged from the army. Deborah went home and eventually married a farmer named Benjamin Gannett. She collected veterans' benefits. After her death, her husband was given a survivor's pension.

**A Mystery From History: The Tecumseh Curse (page 60)**
1. Harrison, pneumonia, 31.
2. Twenty, Lincoln, assassinated.
3. Twenty, Garfield, shot. (assassinated)
4. Twenty, McKinley, shot. (assassinated)
5. Twenty, Harding, died of a stroke.
6. Twenty, Roosevelt, a cerebral hemorrhage.
7. Twenty, Kennedy, assassinated.
8. Twenty, Reagan, shot.

**Civil War Cube Puzzle (page 78)**
Hidden Message: UNCLE TOM'S CABIN

**A Mystery From History: Enlisting in The Army (page 79)**
During the Civil War, many young men, some as young as 16 and 17, wanted to volunteer to fight in the Union army. However, the minimum age for enlisting was 18. Many of these young men were very honest and did not want to lie about their age. They then hit on a plan that would permit them to enlist without lying. They would write the number "18" on a piece of paper and place it in their shoe. Then when the recruiter would ask them how old they were, they could truthfully say, "I'm over 18."

**A Mystery From History: The Mystery of Jesse James (page 84)**
On his way back to town, after the banker had signed the receipt and gotten on his horse, he heard a voice telling him to halt. When he whirled around, he saw four men on horseback. They were wearing masks and their guns were drawn. One of the men searched the banker and found $800. He took the money, and the men rode away. The men, of course, were Jesse James and his gang.

**A Mystery From History: Avoiding Cholera (page 88)**
Joe was correct that by making people on his wagon train drink coffee they could avoid cholera and other diseases. He was wrong, however, when he thought that there was something in the coffee that stopped the disease. It wasn't until 1865 that Louis Pasteur demonstrated that germs caused disease. One of the diseases caused by germs was cholera. We know today that one way to kill germs is to boil water. In order to make coffee, of course, one has to boil water. So it wasn't the coffee, but boiling the water that kept the pioneers healthy.

**Schools in Early America Logic Problem (pages 92–93)**

| Week | Village | Student | Subject Studied |
|---|---|---|---|
| First | Hull | Savannah | Reading |
| Second | Griggsville | Christian | Geography |
| Third | Pittsfield | Henrick | Arithmetic |
| Fourth | Pleasant Hill | Irving | Declamation |
| Fifth | Kinderhook | Edith | Writing |

**Franklin Delano Roosevelt Quotation (page 100)**
Hidden Message: THE ONLY THING WE HAVE TO FEAR IS FEAR ITSELF.

**Lincoln and Kennedy (page 101)**
1. a. Abraham Lincoln was elected to Congress in 1846.
   b. John F. Kennedy was elected to Congress in 1946.
2. a. The name "Lincoln" contains seven letters.
   b. The name "Kennedy" contains seven letters.
3. a. Lincoln was concerned with civil rights.
   b. Kennedy was concerned with civil rights.
4. a. Lincoln was involved in a series of debates.
   b. Kennedy was involved in a series of debates.
5. a. Lincoln was elected President in 1860.
   b. Kennedy was elected President in 1960.

# Answer Keys to Activities

6. a. Lincoln won the election with less than 50 percent of the vote.
   b. Kennedy won the election with less than 50 percent of the vote.
7. a. Lincoln lost a child while living in the White House.
   b. Kennedy lost a child while living in the White House.
8. a. Lincoln had a secretary named Kennedy.
   b. Kennedy had a secretary named Lincoln.
9. a. Lincoln considered not going to the theater where he was assassinated.
   b. Kennedy considered not going to Dallas where he was assassinated.
10. a. Lincoln was shot in the back of the head.
    b. Kennedy was shot in the back of the head.
11. a. Lincoln was shot on Friday.
    b. Kennedy was shot on Friday.
12. a. Lincoln was with his wife when he was assassinated.
    b. Kennedy was with his wife when he was assassinated.
13. a. Lincoln was shot in Ford's Theater.
    b. Kennedy was shot in a Lincoln car, made by the Ford Motor Company.
14. a. Lincoln's assassin was known by three names.
    b. Kennedy's assassin was known by three names
15. a. Lincoln was assassinated by John Wilkes Booth, a Southerner.
    b. Kennedy was assassinated by Lee Harvey Oswald, a Southerner.
16. a. Lincoln's assassin's name has fifteen letters.
    b. Kennedy's assassin's name has fifteen letters.
17. a. Booth ran from a theater and was caught in a barn.
    b. Oswald ran from a warehouse and was caught in a theater.
18. a. Booth was assassinated before his trial.
    b. Oswald was assassinated before his trial.
19. a. Lincoln was succeeded by a Southerner named Johnson.
    b. Kennedy was succeeded by a Southerner named Johnson.
20. a. Andrew Johnson, who succeeded Lincoln, was born in 1808.
    b. Lyndon Johnson, who succeeded Kennedy, was born in 1908.

## Presidential Vanity License Plates (page 106)

1. Washington (Father of our country)
2. Lincoln (Emancipator)
3. Jefferson (Louisiana Buyer)
4. Jackson (Old Hickory)
5. Eisenhower (Ike was his nickname)
6. Carter (Peanut Farmer)
7. Franklin Roosevelt (Four-Time President)
8. Kennedy (PT109 was his ship during WWII)
9. Theodore Roosevelt (Teddy Bear)
10. John Adams (First Adams)
11. Reagan (Actor)
12. Ford
13. Nixon (Watergate)
14. Clinton (Second Impeached)
15. John Quincy Adams (Quincy)

## US (page 107)

1. COLUMBUS
2. GOLD RUSH
3. E PLURIBUS UNUM
4. IN GOD WE TRUST
5. CYRUS MCCORMICK
6. GEORGE BUSH
7. US GRANT
8. MASSACHUSETTS
9. JUSTICE
10. CENSUS
11. MUSKET
12. BUS
13. CUSTER
14. ST. AUGUSTINE
15. RUSSIA

# Answer Keys to Activities

**Famous American Vehicles (page 108)**

| Name of Vehicle | Kind of Vehicle | Description |
| --- | --- | --- |
| Nelson | Horse | George Washington's horse |
| Pueblo | U.S. Navy ship | On January 23, 1968, the *Pueblo* was seized by the North Koreans in the Sea of Japan off the Korean coast. The crew was held captive for 11 months. |
| Titanic | British passenger liner | The *Titanic* struck an iceberg off Newfoundland on the night of April 14–15, 1912, and sank. About 1,500 drowned. |
| Sultana | Steamship | On April 27, 1865, the boiler on the *Sultana* exploded. It was carrying about 2,000 soldiers after the Civil War. Between 1,500 and 1,900 died. |
| Lusitania | British passenger liner | Sunk by a German submarine on May 7, 1915. The incident contributed to the United States' entry into World War I. |
| Hindenburg | German dirigible | While trying to land at Lakehurst, New Jersey, on May 6, 1937, the airship's hydrogen was ignited and the *Hindenburg* was destroyed by fire. Thirty-five of the passengers and crew died, as well as one member of the ground crew. |
| Apollo 11 (Columbia) | Moon rocket (lunar module) | Carried astronauts Neil Armstrong, Edwin "Buzz" Aldrin, and Michael Collins on their historic voyage to the moon and back on July 16–24, 1969. |
| Flyer I | Airplane | The first airplane that Wilbur and Orville Wright flew at Kittyhawk. |
| Enola Gay | Airplane (B-29) | The B-29 that carried the atomic bomb to Hiroshima, Japan. |
| Missouri | U.S. Battleship | World War II formally ended on September 2, 1945, with the formal surrender of Japan aboard the U.S. battleship *Missouri* in Tokyo Bay. |
| Arizona | U.S. Battleship | Sunk by the Japanese in their attack on Pearl Harbor on December 7, 1941, the sunken *U.S.S. Arizona* was dedicated as a national memorial in 1962. |
| Monitor | Ironclad ship | A Civil War ship belonging to the Union. It fought the *C.S.S. Virginia* (originally the *Merrimack*), another ironclad. |
| Merrimack | Ironclad ship | When the Union withdrew from Norfolk in 1861, at the beginning of the war, they sank the *U.S.S. Merrimack*. The Confederates raised the abandoned ship, added an iron casing over the hull and deck, and renamed it the *C.S.S. Virginia*. |
| Constitution | Ship | Called "Old Ironsides," it was one of the original six frigates that made up the U.S. Navy in 1797. |
| Traveler | Horse | General Robert E. Lee's horse |
| Spirit of St. Louis | Airplane | The airplane that American aviator Charles Lindbergh flew when he achieved international fame in 1927 as the first person to fly alone across the Atlantic. |
| Mayflower | Ship | The English ship that carried the Separatist Puritans, later known as Pilgrims, to Plymouth, Massachusetts, in 1620. |
| Niña | Ship | One of Columbus's ships on his first voyage. |

# Answer Keys to Activities

**Many Different Hats of America (page 116)**
1. World War I soldier
2. Cowboy
3. Pilgrim
4. Conquistador
5. Astronaut
6. Abraham Lincoln
7. World War II soldier
8. Confederate soldier
9. Pioneer woman
10. Indian chief
11. Aviator
12. Trapper
13. Marine
14. Minuteman
15. Sailor
16. Pirate

**Scrambled Headlines from the '90s (pages 117–118)**
1. Timothy McVeigh was convicted of the Oklahoma City bombing
2. Madonna gave birth to a daughter, Lourdes Maria Ciccone
3. President Zachary Taylor was exhumed to see if he was poisoned
4. Mike Tyson was disqualified after biting off Holyfield's ear
5. O.J. Simpson was found not guilty of murdering his former wife
6. Tiger Woods was the first nonwhite golfer to win the Masters
7. Christopher Reeve was paralyzed after falling off a horse
8. D. Klebold and Eric Harris killed 11 students, 2 teachers at Columbine High School
9. Flight 800 explodes off Long Island, killing 230
10. John Glenn returned to space aboard the shuttle *Discovery*
11. Mark McGwire broke single-season home run record
12. Tara Lipinski becomes the youngest figure skater to win Olympic gold medal
13. Los Angeles police videotaped beating Rodney King
14. President Clinton was impeached but found not guilty
15. Lisa Marie Presley files for divorce from Michael Jackson
16. Unabomber Ted Kaczynski was arrested for mailing bombs

# Bibliography

Holt, Patricia Lee. *George Washington Had No Middle Name: Little-Known Historical Facts from the Days of the Greeks and Romans to the Present.* Carol Publishing Group,1988.

Erickson, Paul. *Daily Life in a Covered Wagon.* John Wiley & Sons, Inc., 1994.

Bullis, Don, with Robin Shepherd, Editor. *The Old West Trivia Book.* Gem Guides Book Company, 1992.

Seuling, Barbara. *Last Cow on the White House Lawn and Other Little-Known Facts About the Presidency.* Doubleday & Company, Inc., 1978.

Kalman, Bobbie D. *Pioneer Life from A to Z.* Crabtree Publishing Company, 1997.

Pope, John A. Jr., Editor-in-chief. *Strange Stories, Amazing Facts of America's Past.* Readers Digest Association, 1989.

Loewen, James W. *Lies My Teacher Told Me: Everything Your American History Textbook Got Wrong.* The New Press, 1995.

Shenkman, Richard, and Kurt Reiger. *One Night Stands With American History.* Quill, 1982.

Kane, Joseph Nathan. *Famous First Facts.* H. W. Wilson, 1981.

Savage, William W. Jr., Editor. *Cowboy Life: Reconstructing an American Myth.* 1993.

Southworth, Dave. *Gunfighters of the Old West.* Wild Horse Publishing, 1997.

Shenkman, Richard. *I Love Paul Revere Whether He Rode or Not.* HarperCollins Publishers, 1991.

Tuleja, Tad. *Fabulous Fallacies: More Than 300 Popular Beliefs That Are Not True.* Harmony Books, 1982.

Davis, Burke. *The Civil War: Strange and Fascinating Facts.* The Fairfax Press, 1960.

Turner, Geoffrey. *Indians of North America.* Blandford Press Ltd., 1979.

Aron, Paul. *Unsolved Mysteries of American History: An Eye-Opening Journey Through 500 Years of Discoveries, Disappearances, and Baffling Events.* John Wiley & Sons, Inc., 1997.

Editors of American Heritage. *Texas and the War with Mexico.* American Heritage Publishing Company, 1961.

Editors of American Heritage. *The California Gold Rush.* American Heritage Publishing Company, 1961.